PARABLES, BIBLE BUILDING BLOCKS

God's House of Stone

of Stone

Tommy Bruce Jones

INTRODUCTION

For many years parables have been taught their relative meaning with very little attention to their applications. This book's intention is for you to see the parable, its purpose, and its application. Jesus gave these parables to his disciples to understand but not to the people who heard these parables from Jesus (Mat.13:10–11). Jesus wants apostles recognized as teachers of the parables to establish their authority with the people, much like our pastors and teachers of today. Not only does the parable speak of truth in the world but also in a spiritual parallel. But they also reveal future events information to help clarify events by their clues to that event.

Some people refer to parables as made-up stories by Jesus to tell an untrue story to reveal a true spiritual parallel concept. God and /or Jesus does not need to invent a false story as they have all stories from all past individuals (for Judgment Day) and will use a truthful story to make a truthful spiritual percept

I would like you to think of the parables as building blocks for scriptures. If you look at a house in construction, you will see the framing (parables) attached to the foundation. This web of framing (parables) will be the hidden structure for support for the walls and roof. This framing separates each room in the house for distinct functions, and all are tied together. Some rooms are for privacy, some for the community, some for work, and some for-meal preparation. Yet this web holds all together. But this web is hidden from view. Inside it is typically covered by sheetrock, and the exterior is hidden wood, stone, and/or brick. These also are attached to the framing web to give strength and protection to the home occupants. So, it is even with the Bible. Parables will provide a framework revealing many meanings to other scriptures. For example, the parable of the separation of the sheep and Goats adds strength to the Rapture and our actions in this life here on earth.

DEDICATION

I want to dedicate this book to my wife, Dixie, who has been very patient with my time writing the book. Also, I dedicate this book to my son Kerry and my daughter Jill. I pray they both receive a blessing from these words written here.

For my brothers in my prison mission, I hope that you, too, will benefit from my words found here in this book.

PREAMBLE

I also pray for you who read this book that you will benefit from these words. I want you to test my spirit to assure yourself that these words are trustworthy and from God (1 Joh.4:1).

It has been a concern to me for some time that the education of adults has stagnated. We should be learning new and more in-depth information from the Bible as its depths are infinite.

The last Sunday school lesson I was to teach to elders was "*How to Be a Good Citizen.*" This lesson book was word for word for when I was in Sunday school as a teenager. These individuals were 40 to 80+ years old. They should be into the meat and not pabulum.

Our Church education systems need to address the needs of teaching new Christians the Gospel's fundamentals before attending adult classes by age group. This new class should be done by an elder or a deacon or their wives or some knowledgeable individual, on a one-on-one basis until the new Christian has the Gospel foundation to build upon.

For a new Christian, the complicated doctrine can confuse and cause a loss of confidence in their ability to grasp the word. Simplicity to the complicated; adds confidence and surety.

If you feel unsure or overpowered by the words of God, seek out an individual you trust or ask the pastor for an individual who can tutor you in the basics of the Gospel. The Bible is straightforward, but it also can be complicated, too. The Bible reveals a portion of God's mind, and his mind is infinitely greater than ours. Plus, his ways are not our ways (Rom.11:33—36). However, the Holy Spirit knows God's ways and will teach us if we search (Rom.12:1–2).

PRE-PARABLE
INFORMATION

MY CHRISTIAN DICTIONARY

Many words used in scriptures are not capitalized and lose the power and focus of a noun. If I said the words Paris, London, or Chicago, you would focus on those cities. But if I said saints, what power or focus would you have. Therefore, I have capitalized certain christian words. Notice, I spell ½ christian with small letters. This ½ is because our dictionaries do not specifically address the depth of this word Christian.

Humans create our dictionaries, and they do not explain the spiritual meanings in detail. Also, the use of traditional words adds confusion or a lack of understanding in the scriptures.

Here are some simple definitions for the words and the meanings I used in my books.

1. **church** = a group of individuals who believe in God but may not believe in Jesus, or they have performed no works (*deeds*) for Jesus. (*See Pew Sitters*)
2. **Church** = is a group of Christians that have faith in Jesus and perform works *(deeds)* for Jesus
3. ½ christians = **is** a group of individuals who are saved by faith in Jesus but are disobedient to works (deeds) and the Great Commission. *Is half righteous?*
4. **Christians** = are a group of saved persons who are saved by faith and do the works *(deeds)* for the Great Commission. *Righteous*

5. **Pew Sitters** = is a group of individuals who have claimed Jesus and are saved by faith. However, they do not perform works (*deeds*) for the Church or the Great Commission.

6. **The Great Tribulation** = is a name for that time during the seven years of God's greatest wrath against *non-believer* in Jesus.

7. **The Great White Throne Judgment** = is a name for an event during the final day of judgment, by God, for those *non-believers* who will be cast into the Lake of Fire, who come from all the earth's past and comes before the New Earth and New Universe is created and eternity begins.

8. **Hell** = is the Torment location for *non-believers and evil entities,* who are held awaiting the Great White Throne Judgment and the Lake of Fire.

9. **Lake of fire** = is the name of the location for eternal punishment for those *non-believe*rs in Jesus and have blasphemed the Holy Spirit. They come from Hell (Torment) and the Throne Judgment. *Unrighteous*

10. **Torment (Hell)** = is the name of a location that *non-believers* are held awaiting the Great White Throne Judgment.

11. **Paradise** = is the name of 2 locations. One is in the bowls of the earth, and the other is with Jesus in Heaven.

12. **heaven** = is the name of 3 locations: sky, space, and God's abode.

13. **Heaven** = is the place of God's abode and Heaven's Paradise.

14. **Saints** = is a name for all saved individuals. *Righteous*

15. **Old Testament Saints** = is the name of all individuals saved by God' Grace in Old Testament times. Pre and Post Law. *Righteous*

16. **Church Saints** = is a name for all believers in Jesus and who do the Works of Jesus. *Righteous*

17. **Tribulation Saints** = is the name of the individuals who convert to Jesus or who have faith in Jesus and have not received the Mark of the Beast (a mighty deed for the Pew Sitters). During those seven years of the Great Tribulation. *Righteous*

18. **Saved** = is a word for individuals guaranteed salvation by faith, from the Lake of Fire. *Righteous*

19. **Non-believers** = is the name for those who have rejected Jesus as their Lord and Savior. And those who have blasphemed the Holy Spirit. *Unrighteous*

20. **Rapture** = Christians who will be taken to Heaven to avoid the Great Tribulation; but ½ christians (deedless) will miss this treasure.

21. **Our Soul** = is our eternal spiritual body that houses our Spirit.

22. **Our Spirit** = is who we are. Our character, our unseen abilities to understand spiritual concepts, such as Love, beauty, ideas, likes, dislikes, reasoning, forgiveness, and more. This characteristic is especially true in reflecting the light of Jesus.

23. **Our Bodies** = houses our soul, which houses our spirit while present in this carnal state on earth.

24. **god** = is any false god of a pagan religion.

25. **God, GOD** = is our supreme creator, covenant-keeping, and final Judge. The same applies to the Lord and LORD.

26. **Half-Righteous** = is those saved souls by Faith, but who have done nothing (no deeds) for Jesus' Kingdom. They have repented and have been Baptized, come to Church, but <u>have not</u> been obedient to Jesus commands. They are saved by their faith but have no deeds for treasures. One treasure they will miss is the Rapture.
These will be those left behind spoken of in the Bible. During the seven years of the tribulation, they must be obedient to Jesus and work their way to Heaven by NOT accepting the Mark of the Beast. More on this word later.

27. **Living Creatures** = is the name given for aliens. This word alien was used seldom during the Old Testament times, and it never applied to an individual. The word only became popular during Jules Vern's SFI books.

I am sure many will take exception to the words ½ christian or half righteous. This is my attempt to repeal the foundation that causes those that will be left behind. Something has occurred to cause these individuals, who have claimed Jesus as lord, but are not deserving of the Rapture. We see this in Mat. 25:14–30. Matthew Chapters 24 and 25, are Jesus' answer to the apostles' questions about the end of time. And He tells us a parable about Talents. Three men were given talents. It is critical you notice this parable is about ***the kingdom of heaven.*** Two men put their talents to work, and one did not. This is a metaphor for workers in Jesus' Kingdom. The two who works were rewarded with more treasure, but the lazy was denied the treasure. So, this parable reveals the need for deeds for treasure. Also, notice verses 30–31 says,

> **Matthew 25:30–31 *"(30) And cast ye the unprofitable servant into outer darkness: there shall be weeping and gnashing of teeth. (31) When the Son of man shall come in his glory, and all the holy angels with him, then shall he sit upon the throne of his glory:***

In <u>verse 30,</u> notice the lazy servant is cast into darkness, which is into an evil situation (the Great Tribulation)! Which is revealed by, ***"shall be a weeping and gnashing of teeth."*** They realize they have missed the treasure of the Rapture. And now must face the evil deeds of Antichrists #1 and #2.

<u>Verse 31</u> shows Jesus' 3rd Return to establish His Kingdom, is after the weeping and gnashing of teeth. Then if the pew-sitter or the Left Behind or the ½ christians, or the half righteous, will be collected in the 1st Harvest. But only if they have done the deed of rejected the Mark of the Beast.

Hopefully, when you read these words, they will give you focus and directional power in interpreting the scriptures.

SAINTS

D ue to my use of terms, you may not be familiar with, I have included them here for your understanding and clarity in my dissertations.

OLD TESTAMENT SAINTS

So, where are these righteous souls in Noah's time? They are in a place called Paradise. And that it is in the heart of the earth (Mat.12:39–40). You can find this in Luke 16:13–31, the parable of Lazarus and the Rich Man. There are two locations mentioned there, Torment and Paradise.

Abraham was in a righteous place called Paradise with Lazarus, but the unrighteous rich man was in a depraved place called Torment. Now Paradise is where Jesus went after his crucifixion with the thief (Luke 23:43). So, from these verses of scripture, we see two locations, one for the dead righteous individual and one for the deceased unrighteous individual.

Abraham was an Old Testament person, and so was Lazarus; both were saved from Torment. Therefore, they must be considered Old Testament Saints. God's grace saved them by their life's deeds and the condition of their hearts.

The Catholic Church (the first organized denomination) knows many of these righteous individuals they have classified as Saints. And are rightly so but, what of the Saints that have no written evidence of their righteous deeds? What are the names of believers who died in the Roman games, or those Protestants killed during the Dark Ages? Who were the scientists murdered for being heretics because the truth was different than the Pope wanted?

So many individuals were killed (millions) by the powerful unrighteous leaders of the church. And these killings occurred even during the reformation period when the truth was coming forth by many righteous individuals. These are the Old Testaments Saints, before and after the Law was given to man. And how many names of these righteous individuals are not known to be selected by a committee? ***But God and Jesus know them, and they call them Saints.***

We see the church committee named many of these Old Testament righteous people as saints and some New Testament Saints (apostles). But what of the individuals who have performed righteous deeds, even to death, on Jesus' behalf. Do they not deserve to be called Saints? Of course, they deserve that name. But, what of the New Testament righteous individuals who are in Christ?

CHURCH SAINTS

We read in many verses in the New Testament; of individuals called to be Saints (Rom.1).

Romans 1:5–7 *"(5) By <u>whom we have received grace</u> and apostleship, <u>for obedience to the faith among all nations, for his name: (6) Among whom are ye also the called of Jesus Christ:(7) To all that be in Rome,</u> beloved of God, <u>called</u> to be **saints:** Grace to you and peace from God our Father, and the Lord Jesus Christ."*

Notice they (all) were called to be Saints. But, being called does not mean it will be accomplished. However, notice **verse 6**, they are called by Jesus, which means; if you are called by Jesus and accept Jesus as Lord, King, and savior, you will be named a Saint.

This name is spoken to the Church (all believers in Jesus), who will become the Bride of Christ. Only those who believe in Jesus; and are obedient to Jesus' commands (Deeds) will become the Church Saints. And this group of Saints has many unique treasures awaiting them, and one is the Rapture. They will also be Jesus Bride, the Queen of Heaven, rulers with Jesus, and inheriting all things with Jesus. How many righteous Church individuals have died for Jesus; and performed the deeds required by Jesus? Not all are known to us.

The apostles are Saints, but so are John Dow and Marry Smith. Many have served Christ that are unknown to us. But do they not deserve to be called Saints? Of course, they do! Therefore, we have another group of righteous individuals I call the Church Saints. The Church believes in Jesus unto death and performs the deeds required by Jesus. But what of the believer who does not perform deeds?

Remember that treasures have always required deeds. For the Old Testament Saints, they first had the Tree of Knowledge of Good and Evil. God desired for them to do good over evil. But many chose evil, and they had no treasures, just death. But to Noah, his treasure was the ark to Passover God's tribulation on earth, the Flood. This Flood is a precursor of God's tribulation on earth at the end of time and should be celebrated as a Pass Over.

Some of the Church's pew-sitters that do not do the deeds of Jesus; will miss the treasure of the Rapture; and the wedding feast of Jesus and the Bride (The Church). They will need to do the deeds of Jesus during the most perilous of times. See Mat.25.

TRIBULATION SAINTS

Here we see the Tribulation Saints that can be found in many scriptures but not by this name. However, it becomes more apparent as you study scripture. In Mat.22, you will read *The Parable of the Wedding Feast*. This parable runs hand in hand with the Parable of Mat. 25, the 10 Virgins.

In Mat.22, we read of the marriage feast for the king's son. This parable refers to the Marriage of Jesus to his Bride, the Church. Here we see the King as God arranging the Marriage for his son (Jesus). He sends his servants (Prophets) to selected individuals (Jews). They make excuses for not attending (not coming to Jesus' the King's son). The King makes another attempt to call them to the marriage feast by sending his servants (the Apostles). But they kill these servants, just as the apostles were killed.

Over time the preparations for the banquet are ready. But the previously invited (Jews) would not be allowed to come to the marriage of his son (Jesus). God (King) blinded them. Therefore, the king sent his servants to the highways gathered both the good (righteous) and the gentiles to his son's marriage feast. These servants are the apostles, prophets, pastors, laypersons, priests, you, and me, who believe in Jesus for their salvation. They have performed the deeds of gathering the gentiles (lost/bad) to Jesus (Mat.28:18–20).

The gentiles (Christians) gather at the marriage Feast, but one does not have on a wedding garment (white robe – the righteous acts of the Saints) and is tied up and thrown out of the feast.

This person represents the five unprepared virgins who were not permitted into the wedding (the Tribulation Saints). They are saved for eternity but have not performed righteous acts (pew setters). They will go through the Great Tribulation period, and they (Tribulation Saints) will meet Jesus, the Church (Bride of Christ), and the Old Testament Saints at the 1ˢᵗ Harvest of **Rev.14:14–16**. This meeting will be just before the War #1 of Armageddon.

Jesus, the Bride, angels, Tribulation Saint, and Old Testament Saints; will destroy all evil individuals. Those who fall away and accept the Mark of the Beast will eventually be condemned to the Lake of Fire. In Mat.25:1–13, we read of a similar event.

Note

> In Mat.22:13, you will read "*into outer darkness* (evil); "*there shall be weeping and gnashing of teeth.*" This place is not Hell, but the Great Tribulation period of seven years and those unable to enter Jesus' city in Jerusalem during his 1,000-year Kingdom on earth.

> It is not Torment as that is for dead lost souls. And it is not the Lake of Fire as it is also for lost souls, and the pain there will be well beyond the weeping and gnashing of teeth.

HALF CHRISTIAN SAINTS

As I said in my dictionary, you are faced with a new concept word. I created this word is to help explain a more profound knowledge for a reason for the Left-Behind ½ christians. ***They are christians saved by Faith alone.***

However, they are knowingly or not aware of the need for deeds. Deeds, or works, requirement goes all the way back to Adam, and not to eat from the tree, and covertly to use the knowledge of doing good. This requirement was the first test of obedience.

Then came the Law to Moses. It revealed more stringent obedience for salvation. More inference was placed on keeping all the Laws with worship.

When Jesus arrived, he changed requirements to salvation by FAITH. But he created TREASURES by DEEDS. The Great ~~Commission~~ Command was to do the work of bringing souls to Jesus' Kingdom. Another test of obedience. For those Christians who are obedient to Jesus, He gives treasures or rewards.

One of the rewards is a treasure called the Rapture. Without this treasure comes the ½ christians. They are saved by FAITH but perform no deeds for Jesus' Kingdom. They must go through the Great Tribulation; therefore, they are LEFT BEHIND. Now they must perform the act of not excepting the Mark of the Beast (Satan worship). If they accept the Mark, there is no salvation. Their faith is dead. Jam.2:17 and 24.

Some ½ christians may not face the decision to accept or reject the Mark during the seven-year tribulation, and they are saved by faith. When they die during the seven years, they are sent to the Heavenly Paradise and included in the 1st Harvest.

CONTENTS

PARABLE KNOWLEDGE

You must consider all parables as truth, be they about some earthly knowledge or some story. Jesus used parallels to teach from the understood knowledge, to teach about a parallel unknown spiritual knowledge. For example, The Grape Vine. The people knew how to grow grapes and could see the relationship to the spiritual growth for Christians.

Another example is The Rich Man and Lazarus's parable. There God reveals a true story with multiple conceptual meanings. One is how Christians are to help those in need. Another is to show spiritual knowledge about places of the storage of the dead.

Here the good are in Paradise, and evil is in Torment. God knows every story of every person he created and does not need to create a fictional, untrue account! He will recall a perfect non-fiction story that fits his desired outcome.

God hates lies and will not lie to us through an untrue fictional story.

Here I have included a few for your preview so you can see the depth of parables. Too often in the past, we have heard that parables were simple and not too deep in knowledge. And we should not overthink that parable. WRONG, the Bible is full of more in-depth knowledge in all scriptures, so why not the parables? You will see how the parables clarify some future scripture events.

An example is the "Separation of the sheep and goats" and "the Wheat and Tares." Both these concepts point to future events. And in doing so, they help to expand and clarify those future concepts.

CHAPTER 1

The Lost Sheep

Matthew 18:11–14

We find this parable in Matthew 18 and will take us to many new scriptures. Gods is telling us of Jesus' primary missions on earth.

Matthew 18:11 *"For the Son of man is come to save that which was lost."*

This is a quite simple straight forward statement. But is it? What caused God to want to save humanity on earth? Does this include both Jew and Gentiles? Is our planet the only one that has gone to evil? Why now and not before the Flood? Why did not Jesus come when Adam was young and uneducated? Why did not Jesus come and teach Adam and Eve good from evil, like He came and taught us? Why was Jesus not sent to us and reveal God's plan for man?

Even now after 6,000 years we are still unknowing of God plan. He gave us *His primary law that we can do anything we want, and He will let it happen.* He will try to change our thinking by our conscience. Which is proof of the Holy Spirit's present in our life.

God gave us a conscious knowing good from evil. But we have been ignorant of this condition over 5,000 plus years.

There have been times in my life when I felt the pressure to not do a thing but did it anyway.

We can only speculate and make guesses as to God's plan for man. But this verse of scripture reveals God wants everyone on earth in Heaven with him for eternity. Everyone means Jew and Gentile.

Now God askes us a question *"How think ye?"*

Matthew18:12 *"How think ye if a man have an hundred sheep, and one of them be gone astray, doth he not leave the ninety and nine, and goeth into the mountains, and seeketh that which is gone astray?*

So, God uses sheep to make a point. Sheep has been used all through the Bible to refer to Christians

Also, sheep and goats were used for sacrifice on the Hebrew Day of Atonement, for forgiveness for that year's sins. It was for the Hebrew people through the Law given to Moses. So, Jesus used this ceremony to reveal, for the poor, He will take in place of the sheep a Goat for His sacrifice, He will pay for all of earth's people who accept Him as their Lord and savior. For Christians Jew and Gentile on earth.

Now consider the shepherd with his sheep. If the shepherd loses a sheep and goes after the lost, what could happen to those sheep left Behind. They, too, could get lost or lions, bears, or wolves could kill many. Therefore, they must be protected somehow.

Matthew 18 13 *"And if so be that he find it, verily I say unto you, he rejoiceth more of that* sheep, *than of the ninety and nine which went not astray."*

Notice God keeps revealing the Nighty Nine sheep that went not a stray. This is spoken of in numerous scriptures in the Bible. Who with the sin nature of Adam could not go astray? It is planted into our character. Look at our children, we do not have to train them to be evil they drift toward it every day. We have to teach them obedience and other concerns for humanity.

But do not miss this revealing, earth is the sheep that has gone astray. Jesus comes to bring us back into the fold of 99.

If you would like more information on this subject, you can find I in my book *"74 Bible Mysteries Solved"*.

CHAPTER 2

Kingdom is in you

Luke 17:20–37 *"(20) And when he was <u>demanded of the Pharisees, when the kingdom of God should come,</u> he answered them and said, <u>The kingdom of God cometh not with observation:</u> (21) Neither shall they say, Lo here! or, lo there! for, behold, <u>the kingdom of God is within you.</u> (22) And he said unto the disciples, The days will come, when ye shall desire to see one of the days of the Son of man, and ye shall not see it. (23) And they shall say to you, See here; or, see there: go not after them, nor follow them. (24) <u>For as the lightning, that lighteneth out of the one **part** under heaven, shineth unto the other **part** under heaven; so shall also the Son of man be in his day.</u> (25) <u>But first must he suffer many things, and be rejected of this generation. (26) And as it was <u>in the days of Noe, so shall it be also in the days of the Son of man.</u> (27) They did eat, they drank, they married wives, they were given in marriage, until the day that Noe entered into the ark, and the flood came, and destroyed them all. (28) Likewise also as it was in the days of Lot; they did eat, they drank, they bought, they sold, they planted, they builded; (29)But the same day that Lot went out of Sodom it rained fire and brimstone from heaven, and <u>destroyed</u> them all. (30) Even thus shall it be in the day when the <u>Son of man</u> is revealed."*

This parable is a comparison type as Jesus uses a comparison between the world conditions in Noe's day to reveal the same circumstances that will disclose the time of Jesus' 2nd Return to earth. He initially needs to announce his kingdom's initial location, which he will bring with him on his 3rd Return.

The *clue* in verse 20 reveals that Jesus' initial kingdom is not visual but a covert intimate internal kingdom. The Church.

THE INTERNAL KINGDOM

Verse 21 has an obvious *clue* revealed to us, and it says, *"the Kingdom of God is within you."* And not to be confused with Jesus' 1,000-year Kingdom, which will be headquartered in Jerusalem. This knowledge is not a news flash for Christians; we know that we are placed into Christ and Christ into us when we accept Jesus as our Lord and savior.

This transfer of Jesus (the King) into our lives comes without fanfare and visual proof. The Holy Ghost is called a ghost because he is spirit and not visible, but his results, by his actions, can be seen revealing that person's changed lifestyle. Many scriptures are showing this merging of our spirit with Jesus' spirit (1st John 2:24). Notice in verse 24, the two clues of remaining *"IN the son and IN the father."*

Verse 22 moves ahead in time to a point where the days of righteousness will be desired but will not be. Notice Jesus is speaking to his disciples, those that serve Jesus, and not necessarily his apostles. Jesus uses disciples to include apostils, disciples, and Christians; all are serving Jesus.

However, disciples infer a continuation unto the future. If this pertains to some point in the future, it appears to be speaking of the Great Tribulation. There the left behind (saved by Faith with no deeds) will desire the return to the time of the Church. But the Church has been Raptured to Jesus. God's seven-year tribulation is taking its toll on the left behind ½ christians.

The words *"the days of the son of man"* points to that spiritual condition during Jesus' walk on earth. It was a time of new enlightenment, an increase of Biblical knowledge, hope into a new way of salvation, security in God during troubling times, people experiencing love on a grander scale as never before. Heaven revealed on earth, and who would not want that to be?

Also, Verse 22 gives a *clue* and an answer to that *clue*. In the Tribulation Saints' desires, they want the son of man, Jesus, to come quickly. We see this in Rev. 6:9–11, where the souls under the alter (Tribulation Saints) cry out in a loud voice,

"How long, O Lord, holy and true, dost thou not judge and avenge our blood?" But God answers them with, wait until their brothers are killed as they were killed (beheaded). Then the movement to the understanding of this delay is revealed in **verse 23.**

Verse 23 and 24 answers their loud cry *"How long"* by the statement *which is not about the thief in the night* but of a point in time that will be of such a great magnitude that it will be unmistakably clear it is Jesus' 3rd Return to destroy evil and establish his 1,000-year Kingdom. We will read next that this event is into the future of this scripture.

Verse 25 speaks of a time future to Luke, where Jesus must suffer and be rejected by his generation. Jesus was tortured and crucified on the cross, for a crime he did not commit, and with an illegal verdict, by an unlawful evil religious Court. But next, Jesus will give us a *clue* as to the time of Jesus coming back to earth as King.

Verse 26 starts a dialogue to give us a time of Jesus' 3rd Return. This dialogue is also supported by Daniel 12. Notice that the son of man's (Jesus) return will be as it was in Noah's day. So, this *clue* will take two verses of scripture to understand this statement fully. The first verse is found in Gen. 6

Genesis 6:5 *"And GOD saw that the wickedness of man* **was great in the earth and** that *every imagination of the thoughts of his heart* **was only evil continually.** *"*

Notice --- their thoughts were continually evil. Remember, they were given the knowledge of good vs. evil, and it is obvious they chose evil so often; it became normal in their daily life. Now let us look at another scripture, Mat. 24:36–39, which gives us additional information.

Matthew 24:36–39 *"(36) But of that day and hour knoweth no* man, *no, not the angels of heaven, but my Father only. (37) But as the days of Noe* were, *so shall also the coming of the Son of man be. (38) For as in the days that were before the flood they were eating and drinking, marrying and giving in marriage, until the day that Noe entered into the ark, (39) And knew not until the flood came, and took them all away; so shall also the coming of the Son of man be."*

First, notice the *clue* in verse 36 pertains to the Rapture (Jesus' 2nd Return). I say this because, in Daniel 12, God gave him the exact day of Jesus' 3rd Return. Therefore, the Rapture will come like a thief in the night (unnoticed). In comparison to Jesus' 3rd Return, this will be spectacular! And not like a thief in the night.

Then consider verse 37. We looked at Gen. 6:5 first, which reveals evil continually but look at verses 38. There you will read of normal, acceptable daily events occurring. These verses show that the people in Noah's time considered evil as their everyday mental attitude. Even during normal day-to-day activities, they were continually thinking of evil during events that should be joyous.

Also, in verse 39, notice how they continue their evil way for 120 years while Noah built the Ark and preached the coming tribulation (flood). The Ark was a visual sign of the coming flood, just as the increase of evil is a *clue* for ½ christians of the Great Tribulation's coming.

Can you see this occurring today? Modern-day prophets are preaching of the coming of Jesus to Rapture his Bride, the Church. And this event will catch many ½ christians sleeping (no deeds). These sleepers are saved by Faith but have missed the treasure of the Rapture. The final *clue* is the thief catches them in the night as they are not looking for *clues* to Jesus' 2nd Return, which they were told to do so in the Bible. Obedience?

As it was in Noah's time, it is remarkably close to our time. Evil is proliferating. Satan's covert worship is the next *clue,* but today the *clue* is the Church, the Bride of Christ, and the Church of Laodicea, becoming increasingly self-centered. If we are saved by faith, why do the deeds required of Jesus (disobedience)? I can spend that time and effort and make more money. Traditions have smothered the new truths becoming known. But the truth of the gospel is unchanged.

LESSONS LEARNED

1. When we accept Jesus, he comes to live in us through the Holy Spirit.
2. With Jesus in us, and he is the King of Kings, and His Kingdom will last forever, we have an eternal internal spiritual kingdom.
3. That Kingdom is under the protection of Jesus and God.
4. There is nothing that can remove that Kingdom from us, except us. Stay strong, run the race, be faithful to Jesus, and love all.
5. Be patient, wait for your answer prayers to be answered but keep in mind:

Romans 8:18, "*For I reckon that the sufferings of this present time* are not worthy to be compared with the glory which shall be revealed in us."

Romans 8:38–39 "*(38) For I am persuaded, that neither death, nor life, nor angels, nor principalities, nor powers, nor things present,*

nor things to come, (39) Nor height, nor depth, nor any other creature, shall be able to separate us from the love of God, which is in Christ Jesus our Lord".

Question, for what are you willing to die?

Death and taxes are a guarantee. We all face death possibilities. To accept a painful death, you must prepare yourself ahead for that event to go through the pain or find a way to escape.

CHAPTER 3

Lamp Under the Bowl

Matthew 5:14–16 *"(14) <u>Ye are the light of the world.</u> A city that is set on an hill cannot be hid. (15) Neither do men light a candle, and put it under a bushel, but on a candlestick; and it giveth light unto all that are in the house. (16) Let your light so shine before men, that they may see your good works, and glorify your Father which is in heaven."*

<u>Verse 14</u> is the <u>1st clue</u> that reveals we Christians are reflectors of Jesus' light of righteousness. We that Jesus saves are to reflect, by our visual actions, the righteousness we show by those actions. We are not to hide our righteous light but to place it in a position for all individuals to see Jesus.

- This scripture should reveal that we are not to hide our light to the world as there are lost souls seeking meaning for their lives. Out proof of being a dependable beacon of light will place Jesus into their thoughts for consideration. If we do not remain stable, they will not see the more profound truth of our faith. These words will be the most challenging task for the Tribulation Saints during the Great Tribulation.
- Jesus supported this concept with his death on the cross. Jesus could have called millions of angels down to save him from this painful death, but he did not. We Christians, too, must resolve to die also if needs be. We know our destination is Heaven. But

those who are not determined and fall away are destined to the Lake of Fire.

<u>Verse 15</u> is the <u>*2nd clue*</u> that supports this concept of not hiding your light before man.

- When we need light to light our way in the darkness, we turn on a light, be it a lamp or a flashlight, so we do not trip and fall or bump into something and get hurt. We take this need without a thought about the light of Jesus to reveal unrighteousness obstacles in our way in this life. Therefore, our light can be a guide for all those souls around us.
- Christians, in particular, are being observed without our noticing it. The lost are looking for something that reveals and fills the vacancy in their life. They know there is more to life than their meager existence. Some revert to one-night stands; others dedicate their lives to their work. Many individuals are afraid to ask Christians about Jesus because their friends will ridicule them in front of others. They are not aware that a <u>*true friend*</u> would not perform this embarrassment to them, especially in front of others.

<u>Verse 16</u> is the <u>*3rd clue,*</u> which now combines both 14 and 15 into a very poignant statement about the dedicated Christian's actions we are to perform. Christians are to show the power of Jesus in our consistent reflecting Jesus light, especially in fearful and terrifying times. Death is especially one. The faith in Jesus' power of salvation will be the most difficult for Tribulation Saints to sustain their position in Jesus' eternal life. Satan will use this against the Tribulation Saints and some of us on earth. Many missionaries and fellow believers have been put to death for not denying Jesus. And this atrocity is happening today all over the earth. And some have fallen away. 2nd Thes. 2.

2ⁿᵈ Thessalonians 2:3–4 *"(3). Let no man deceive you by any means: for* that day shall not come, <u>except there come a falling away first, and that man of sin be revealed, the son of perdition;</u> *(4) Who opposeth and exalteth himself above all that is called God, or that is worshipped; <u>so that he as God sitteth in the temple of God,</u> shewing himself that he is God."*

These events will happen in the last days! Look for it. Satan has always wanted to be like God, and he will, to a limited extent, achieve this desire during the last 3½ years of the seven years of the Great Tribulation.

God's ways are not our ways. To remain stable even in times of confusion and in negative wonderment. *Why God? Where are you, God? Why this little one, Lord?* All will become clear in time. Keep the faith in Jesus' love for you.

LESSON LEARNED

1. God does not want you to hide your light of Jesus during troubling times.
2. He wants your strength over Satan and yourself, so you can be the inspiration for the weak and lost.
3. Your reflected light actions and faith in Jesus will be the proof for those weak and lost that Jesus is the way into eternity.

Matthew 5:14--16 *"(14) Ye are the light of the world. A city that is set on an*

hill cannot be hid. (15) Neither do men light a candle, and put it under a bushel, but on a candlestick; and it giveth light unto all that are in the <u>house</u>. (16) Let your light so shine before men, that they may see your good works, and glorify your Father which is in heaven."

4. The weak, fallen away Christians will fully understand, their total commitment to Jesus is necessary. (deeds)

5. To the left behind, hiding your light reveals a total lack of trust in God, which can only be overcome by denying the Mark of the Beast in public during the Great Tribulation. A personally, most demanding deed to overcome, in a hideous death.

6. The *unhidden lamplight* of your life will reap great treasures, which will remain with you to enjoy forever.

7. *Death is a foregone conclusion*, so decide NOW in advance: *"What are you willing to die for, good or evil?"*

<u>Do not deceive yourself; prepare for eternity!</u>

CHAPTER 4

Foolish and the Wise Builders

Matthew 7:24–27 *"(24) Therefore whosoever heareth these sayings of mine, and doeth them, I will liken him unto a wise man, which built his <u>house</u> upon a rock: (25) And the rain descended, and the floods came, and the winds blew, and beat upon that house; and it fell not: <u>for it was founded upon a rock.</u> (26) And every one that heareth these sayings of mine, and doeth them not, shall be likened unto a foolish man, which built his house upon the sand: (27) And the rain descended, and the floods came, and the winds blew, and beat upon that house; and it fell: and great was the fall of it."*

Here we read to build our house (our soul) strong to withstand Satan's attacks. This sounds like the Three Little Pigs story. Where they each were to build their house strong to survive an attack by the Big Bad Wolf.

This effort primarily starts with your mind. *Just for what are you willing to die?* We all will die (except for those Raptured, 2nd Return), so what are you ready to die for; Heaven or the Lake of Fire?

If you select Heaven (Sheep), be prepared to experience the attacks of Satan. For those Saints (goats) going through the Great Tribulation, you must expect Satan to pressure you with all sorts of hideous temptations. And it will be only with your knowledge of scripture as to the results or consequence of your actions, which will assure you salvation. Therefore, you must build your spiritual strength strong to with-stand Satan or demons attacks.

Deeds have and always will be required for treasures. Those saved by *faith but without deeds,* who are alive at Jesus 2nd Return (separation of Sheep and goats) will not be Raptured. They (goats) will go through the Great Tribulation and *will be required not to fall away*

To *fall away* reveals your faith in Jesus is not within you. You do not believe Jesus can save you from eternal Death. Here is the challenge for which you must be prepared.

So, I ask, *"what are you willing to die for"? You can only get this strength through the study of God's words and prayer.* If you do not have this strength and accept the Mark of the Beast (Satan) and give your worship to Satan and not Jesus (God), *there is no hope for you.* If you do not accept the Mark, you or your family will be killed before your very eyes. If you do not know their destination after death, you will succumb to Satan's attack. Accepting the Mark will guaranty your place in the Lake of Fire.

I must include a *caveat here;* however, be careful depending on it as it may rely heavily on the actual condition of your heart. A person whose heart is willing to go to the Lake of Fire to save their loved ones may find God's mercy. However, remember those too, who you are ready to sacrifice for, will face the same decision to accept or reject the Mark of the Beast themselves. If they accept the Mark your sacrifice was for naught.

Some Pew-Sitter may NOT meet this challenge of the Mark of the Beast and die of old age or sickness during these seven years. Their faith will save them. But remember, do not deceive yourself. Do not hang on to that old way of putting things off until the last minute. Get busy with Jesus' work and do commands, deeds.

In <u>verse 25,</u> we see that the house, going through troubles, is not built on the Rock. Its foundation is not secure and well stationary. This Rock represents Jesus, as Jesus is called the Rock many times in the Bible (Psl. 18:15/27; 1st Cor. 10).

1st Corinthians 10:4 *"And did all drink the same spiritual drink: for they drank of that spiritual Rock that followed them: <u>and that Rock was Christ.</u>"*

There is another verse of scripture that reveals Jesus is a stumbling stone Rom.9.

Roman 9:31–33 *"(31) But Israel, which followed after the law of righteousness, hath not attained to the law of righteousness. (32) Wherefore? Because* **they sought it** *not by faith but as it were by the works of the law. For they stumbled at that stumblingstone; (33) As it is written, Behold, I lay in Sion a stumblingstone and rock of offence: and whosoever believeth on him shall not be ashamed."*

Here we read of the Hebrews who stumbled over Jesus and held to the Law of Moses for salvation and still do today, if at all. This verse of Roman refers to Isaiah as it was written by Isaiah 9:14–15. Isaiah's writing occurred around 760 BC, well before Jesus in 5 BC.

LESSONS LEARNED

1. The building of the house here is referring to our house that houses our eternal soul.
2. This house needs to be correctly built to withstand rain, wind, and other natural and spiritual tragedies.

3. This parable is for all Christians at all times. But it will become especially true for those deedless ½ christians left behind. Their past house was not built on the Rock, and now you will need to secure your house (soul) on the deeds required by God to make your home secure.

4. You cannot sit in the pews and do nothing for the Church and lost souls. Mat. 28 is a command, not a commission.

5. Your lack of deeds should reveal the condition of your heart. Example: do you fully understand what Jesus did for you. He died for you; are you willing to repay him in kind? Do you grasp the magnitude of love God has for you? Do you feel the need to return your love to God? Do you study God's word with an eager heart? Are you willing to forgive others?

6. Now in Mat. 28, Jesus commands us to go and teach Jesus Gospel unto all the nations. *Notice this is not a ~~Commission~~ but an order (command).*

Mathew 28:19–20 *"(19) Go ye therefore, and teach all nations, baptizing them in the name of the Father, and of the Son, and of the Holy Ghost: (20) Teaching them to observe all things whatsoever **I have commanded you**: and, lo, I am with you alway, even unto the end of the world. Amen."*

America is a nation too.

When this verse of scripture was written, America was not a nation. It was tribal by natural events. Therefore, we need to convert all of America, too. It is reasonable service for Jesus to continue in His footsteps of spreading the Gospel.

CHAPTER 5

Seeds Sown

Matthew 13:3–9 *"(3) And when he sowed, some **seeds** fell by the way side, and the fowls came and devoured them up:(5) Some fell upon <u>stony places</u>, where they had not much earth: and forthwith they sprung up, because they had no deepness of earth: (6) And when the sun was up, they were scorched; and because they had no root, they withered away. (7) And some fell among <u>thorns</u>; and the thorns sprung up, and choked them: (8) But other fell into <u>good ground</u>, and brought forth fruit, some an hundredfold, some sixtyfold, some thirtyfold. (9) Who hath ears to hear, let him hear."*

I would like you to consider the last sentence first. *"Who hath ears to hear, let him hear."* What is Matthew trying to convey to us? These previous verses are revealing a critical point. They have a deeper meaning of a spiritual truth, which will parallel this practical truth.

The seed represents the seed of the words of knowledge. That has been sent into our brain by a pastor, friends, and/or the Bible. Then the following verses reveal the condition of that person's mind and heart that receives these words. Do they understand it with their brain, and is their heart moved to spread the gospel to the lost souls? The heart is the challenge for the hearer. If you are reading this book, *you are hearing*!

<u>Verse 5</u> gives us our first metaphoric *clue of stony places*. As you are aware, the stones are extremely hard. Most natural elements cannot

penetrate the hard stone. However, you will see roots growing over a hard rock because that rock was initially covered with soil where the root diverted over the rock in that soil. But erosion eventually eroded that topsoil away, leaving the long root. This metaphor can reveal God's words can be given to a hard-headed individual who might start to consider the truth, but friends mock him into rejecting the words.

Verse 6 pertains to strength to maintain longevity in Christ. For this strength, we must continue in our study in scripture and remain in the fellowship of believers. If we avoid these, we will forget their value they give to our life. And become a target for Satan. This lack of strength and Satan's attack will cause some to fall away from Jesus.

Like an athlete who must practice and study the coach's plan, so must we also do. Strength is retained by doing the works.

The 2ⁿᵈ *clue* is in verse 7 of those who readily receive the words and attend church, but never seem to study or cherish God's words, and it soon becomes more of a burden. They have no roots down into the structure of God's Love and plan for their lives. Eventually, trials and light repercussions come, and they have no knowledge or strength to deal with it. They blame God! How could a loving God allow this to happen to me or my loved one?

Plants need water, and without it, they die, and the same with the person that does not study God's word. They cannot believe all things work together for good to those who God loves. They appear to think that once they have accepted Jesus, all will be pleasant and protected from serious harm. This concept is due *to old traditions* they have heard, and they have not read the Bible thoroughly. If they had, they would know that trials will come, but they are protected from Hell and eventually the Lake of Fire. You need roots to survive!

A plant without roots will die. Without the roots seeking nourishments, it is like our lack of seeking spiritual nourishment. We need the words of God to remain strong and to grow in strength.

The thorns are metaphoric to the everyday problems we encounter. The thorns are painful trivial things that cause much discomfort. These represent our existence globally, be it job, family, weather, disasters, death, and many other daily trials we face. It is our attitude that affects us the most.

Accidents and death are challenging emotions to overcome or understand. We look at *our loss* rather than the *joy our loved ones gave when alive.* But now they are with Jesus and out of pain. *It is tough to overcome our heartbreak. And to realize and praise God for the time we were privileged to have had with that loved one.* And for believers, our loved ones have run their race and *are waiting with God for you* when you finish your race.

Our genuine painful concern should be for those without hope of salvation. We cannot fathom the eternal Lake of Fire's pain, which is the final destination for a non-believer in Jesus. As there is no other name in Heaven, whereby we must be saved!!!!!!!

Acts 4:12 Neither is there salvation in any other: for there is none other name under heaven given among men, whereby we must be saved."

<u>Verse 8</u> reveals the excellent ground, soil with nutrition for the seeds to germinate and grow. Add water (people, nations, and tongues), and the seeds will grow and yield much more than one seed. And each new seed, in turn, will mature and produce more fruit.

<u>Verse 9</u> ends with the statement, *"Who hath ears to hear, let him hear."* We know every person has an ear, but some cannot hear, but they can

read. Even the blind today can see with the use of brail. But what this statement is saying is, if you receive God's word, then listen to it. If you refuse God's word and let it not penetrate your consciousness, it will depart from that person. But a verse in the Bible says his words will not return void Isa.55:11.

Isaiah 55:11 *"So shall my word be that goeth forth out of my mouth: it shall not return unto me void, but it shall accomplish that which I please, and it shall prosper* in the thing **whereto I sent it.**

So, you think you have nothing to speak to others about Jesus, remember you have received the words, and the Holy Spirit will lead you with the words you have to influence that person in some way. Every little thing you do for Jesus' Kingdom will not be forgotten. So have faith even in your hour of doubt, but remember, as you study, you will become more secure in your knowledge God will give you. Treasures await you in Heaven.

LESSONS LEARNED

1. The seeds sown are words, thoughts, ideas, doctrine, actions, and commands given by God's Bible to his people.
2. The ground is human beings, which hear the words of the sown seeds. Jesus reveals to us the diverse types of soil, or people, who hear his words and their reactions we can expect.
3. Those who have been genuinely saved in Jesus are born a new creature but still have sinful nature. We know we need the word of God to be able to grow in Christ and overcome our nature and Satan. Without this knowledge and faith in Jesus, we cannot reject the Mark of the Beast.
4. We know or should know that all things work for the good of those who love and trust in God.

5. Without this knowledge, Christians and those lost souls could hate God, and they will have an eternal painful emotional and physical existence.

6. It is our responsibility to spread the gospel of Jesus. If we commoners do not do it, who will? Remember, too; we are included in the Great Command to teach all nations and make disciples.

CHAPTER 6

The Widow's Judgment

Luke 18:1–8 *"(1) And he spake a parable unto them to this end, that men ought always to pray, and not to faint; (2) Saying, There was in a city a judge, which feared not God, neither regarded man: (3) And there was <u>a widow</u> in that city; and she came unto him, saying, <u>Avenge me</u> of mine <u>adversary</u>. (4) And <u>he would not</u> for a while: but afterward he said within himself, Though I fear not God, nor regard man; (5) Yet because this widow troubleth me, I will avenge her, lest by her continual coming she weary me. (6) <u>And the Lord said, Hear what the unjust judge saith.</u> (7) And shall not God avenge his own elect, <u>which cry day and night</u> unto him, though he bear long with them? (8) I tell you that he will avenge them speedily. <u>Nevertheless, when the Son of man cometh, shall he find faith on the earth?</u>"*

"How think ye?" Does this parable seem simple on the surface? The unjust judge mistreated the widow, right? But this answer makes several assumptions based on traditions.

One tradition is our experience with widows, and another is our experience with unjust authorities. Our life experiences initially motivate us. For example: was your widowed grandmother a kind, sweet, elderly, and loving lady? Have you been unjustly treated by your parents (or an authority) at some time in your early past? If so, it will affect your thought patterns in self-defense and protection mechanisms within your unconscious awareness.

This self-protection causes complicated issues for us, but God has given us information to simplify the process. So let us look at the foundations of justice.

1. God has given us the Knowledge of Good and Evil through Adam's sin; we call it our conscience.
2. God has given us the Laws for our carnal society's survival. And on appropriate punish for broken Laws.
3. God gave us Laws for our spiritual survival.
4. God Gave us Laws to reveal to us what is sin.
5. God has given us the rewards for obedience to those Laws.

So, it seems appropriate to me we should base our correct decisions on these faithful foundations. Therefore, the foundation is:

1. Our conscience is the working of the Holy Spirit in our daily lives. He tries to motivate us to do good over evil. Some people call it a gut feeling and see the devil on one shoulder preaching evil and an angel on the other shoulder preaching good, both trying to influence us.
2. The social Laws give us the specific law and also for that disobedience to that law' punishment. If you study the first five books of the Bible, you will find a particular law and God's specific punishment for breaking that law. These laws pertain to man's existence on earth, even during Jesus' Kingdom of 1,000 years. *("Not one jot or tittle will depart from the Law").*
3. Here God reveals to man the perfection required to be with God for eternity. Man is human (carnal), and this law pertains to the spiritual requirements to exercise by physical, mortal man, but it is impossible for carnal man, but not the mortal son of man (Jesus).

4. It is in God's plan to reveal to his elect what defines sin. A pre-law man had no guidelines as to these laws, and they regressed into evil. This regression, too, was in God's plan to reveal that we will also revert to evil without some guidance. It became necessary to explain just what defines sins. We see this exact reversion of Preflood man today, with the increase of wickedness and Jesus's rejection.

5. If we attempt to be obedient to God and Jesus and put our faith and efforts towards good, God will bless those obedient with unimaginable eternal treasures.

We can understand justice and we know there is *mortal punishment*, and there is *eternal spiritual punishment.* If we are to judge angels in Jesus' Kingdom, we need to take this parable as a lesson. Always remember Jam.1.

James1:19–20 *"(19) Wherefore, my beloved brethren, let every man be <u>swift to hear, slow to speak, slow to wrath</u>: (20) <u>For the wrath of man worketh not the righteousness of God</u>".*

There are two avenues of considerations in this parable. One the widow is unrighteous, and the other she is righteous? So let us look at the possibility of an unrighteous widow.

THE UNRIGHTEOUS WIDOW

The 1ˢᵗ *clue* is in verse 2; the judge has no regard for man or God. The 2ⁿᵈ *clue* is in verse 3, why did the widow come to an unjust judge for justice? The 3ʳᵈ *clue* is in verse 3 is, does she want vengeance *(Vengeance is mine saith the lord).* The 4ᵗʰ *clue* is the apparent lack of justice or an unjust verdict on her claim. The 5ᵗʰ *clue* is the lack of knowledge in which the judge rendered this decision. The 6ᵗʰ *clue* is in verse 6, where the widow brings trouble to the judge *(Love your neighbor as yourself).*

The *7ᵗʰ clue* is in verse 6, hear the judge change the verdict to avenge and appease the widow (Mat.18:6). *The 8ᵗʰ clue is in verse 7, is not God the avenger of the elect (Rom.12:19)?* Then in verse 7, God reveals *clue 9*, which seems out of place. *"Nevertheless, when the Son of man cometh, shall he find faith on the earth?"*

Please notice this verse references Jesus' 3ʳᵈ return, and *he will find Faith on the earth*. More on this subject will come later.

Notice this judge had no regard for man, just the Law. And this widow came to him for *justice or was it for vengeance.* So let us look into our understanding of a *Biblical widow as it challenges our traditions of just what constitutes is a widow.* By tradition, we believe a widow is a person whose husband has died. And that is partly correct. However, the inference to this tradition is for all women and *is not entirely accurate 1ˢᵗ Tim.5.*

1ˢᵗ Timothy 5:9–11; 14; 16 "*(9) Let not a widow be taken into the number under threescore years old,* having been the wife of one man, *(10) Well reported of for good works; if she have brought up children, if she have lodged strangers, if she have washed the saints' feet, if she have relieved the afflicted, if she have diligently followed every good work. (11) But the younger widows refuse: for when they have begun to wax wanton against Christ; they will marry"; (14) I will therefore that the younger women marry, bear children, guide* the house, give none occasion to the adversary to speak reproachfully. *(16) If any person that believeth have widows, let them relieve them, and let not the Church be charged;* that it may relieve them that are widows indeed. "

These verses have been a thorn in women's sides for a long time. What a challenging time early in the death of a husband, especially in the New Testament times for young mothers. Here Timothy is trying to protect both young widows and old widows and *the local Church resources for widows.* The Church is responsible for their widows' care within that Church body, and not the government. A widow would be accountable to that Church's members, where the government, just by excessive vast spread numbers of widows, cannot properly monitor their qualifications and conditions.

Timothy is also concerned with young mothers who may get accustomed to the Church, providing long-term support for the young widow, to the loss of support for the older true *indeed* widows. Most Churches, even today, cannot support young mothers for the long term. Old windows have no or very chance to find a new husband or work, where younger widows do have this possibility.

Notice Timothy's first *clue* is 60 years old (*under threescore years*). The second *clue* is *"the wife of one man."* This clue appears to be for the woman who is not part of a harem and has never been married before this husband died. However, this last idea has some holes in it in the Bible. One, what if the woman's husband was a soldier and he was killed in battle? Under the old law, she was to marry his brother. Would this prevent her from Church help if she remarried and her second husband died in an accident? What if a woman married an unbeliever who divorced his wife, but then he died? Other verses in the Bible relieve the woman of her marriage vow. See Num. 30 and Deu.24:1–2.

Notice this widow persisted in coming back and back and back to this judge, insisting on her justice (vengeance?). This judge is not an honorable man. The *clue* is given in <u>verse 6</u>, *"<u>And the Lord said, Hear what the unjust judge saith</u>."*

This judge has given into this persistent women's possible wrongful claim at the expense of the other potential righteous victim's claim. God is revealing to us that injustice is in this world until Jesus' 3rd Return. It is then Jesus will destroy all evil individuals and cast them into Hell

(Torment) quickly. We will see our long or short wait for justice, which will be revealed to those who have received injustice in this life.

Can you just imagine all the Jews and gentiles murdered by Hitler, standing and seeing Hitler and his henchmen cast screaming into The Lake of Fire? Be patient, brothers; God will call everyone into account for their life's work. They may get away with crimes on earth but not from God.

Verse 7 makes a fascinating statement! These individuals appear to be the Tribulation Saints found under the altar (Rev.6:9–10). These Tribulation Saints are those from the seven years of The Great Tribulation who have not accepted the Mark of the Beast. They have been beheaded for their faith in Jesus by not accepting the Mark of the Beast. This condition is supported by the following verse 8.

Verse 8, in many ways, has been overlooked. The vital *clue* here is, nevertheless, *"when the Son of man cometh, shall he find faith on the earth?"* Please note, this is a question and not a statement. Will Jesus find faith on the earth? *"How think ye?"* The answer is YES!

This answer will require our knowledge of past and future prophecies. It will require knowledge we should have found in our study with the help of the Holy Spirit. Plus, God has chosen those who he desires to have the privilege to reveal that knowledge (the 144.000). So *"How think ye"? "Change the verdict or not"?*

THE RIGHTEOUS WIDOW

A Judge must consider all sides of a problem to develop the correct answer. The unrighteous widow is a possibility and a substantial consideration. And more evidence is against her. However, to thoroughly understand the situation, we must also look at the other side, no matter how erroneous it initially appears. We may have missed a *clue* that could change the complexion of the problem.

If we return the Luke 18:1, we read, pray, and not faint. But God uses the concept of judging to reveal the parallel spiritual truth for continual prayer. That way, we will need to know about judging to grasp the concept of continual prayer. In 1st Thes. 5, we read:

1st Thessalonians 5:17–21 "(17) *Pray without ceasing. (18) In everything give thanks: for this is the will of God in Christ Jesus concerning you. (19) Quench not the Spirit. (20) Despise not prophesyings. (21) Prove all things; hold fast* that which is good."

We have several *clues* listed here in these verses, and they are:

1. Pray continually.
2. Give thanks for all situations; God is in control.
3. Listen to the Holy Spirit.
4. Do not reject scriptures, especially prophecy.
5. Prove all things: Test the Spirit (1st John 4).
6. Stay faithful, hold fast, to righteousness.
7. Apply God's Laws to the problem.

With these above thoughts, let us now look into this parable with this new information. And the *1st clue* is to pray continually. Notice no mention of the widows praying. How is this constant prayer possible when we engage in intense work when our minds need to lock into our every movement? How can a brain surgeon pray during intense brain surgery?

We know multifunctioning can cause errors in driving a car, which is an intensive task. However, we can pray for momentary problems or success. If you are late to work and properly driving the speed limit, and catch a green light, thank the Lord. If you catch a red light, praise the

Lord too, and now you have time for a moment of longer prayer time. Ask for forgiveness for being late. The point is when an opportunity presents itself; we should be of the attitude to want to be in prayer with our father. Now let us look into this widow's request.

Without any information to the contrary, this widow is called a widow. She meets all the requirements, of a Bible, for a righteous widow (1st Tim. 5). She is seeking justice for an unjust verdict for her. Instead of her adversary, or there had been no verdict given yet. But notice, she is seeking *vengeance* from a judge that does not fear God. *" avenge of my adversary."*

Vengeance is not permitted by New Testament Christians (Rom.19:19). But this parable is occurring before Jesus comes to earth. However, revenge was allowed by the Kinsman Redeemer (avenger) in the Old Testament (Num. 35:6–33). But this widow has no Kinsman Redeemer. Therefore, she must speak for herself.

She chooses a judge that fears not God or no man. This judge is an independent thinker. She wants him to be her Kinsman Redeemer (her avenger) but, he will not avenger her. It is in her continuous repetition that the judge finally gives in.

If this parable's foundation is about prayer for today (New Testament), then the judge of our time is either Jesus or God. But can either Jesus or God be cajoled into situations against God's desires or plans? NO! Our prayers always have three answers, which are:

1. YES ----- *but wait. If it is granted immediately, there will be no delay or minimal delay.*
2. NO ---- *no [or not at this time].*
3. YOU GOT TO BE KIDDING -------- !

We see the answer YES immediately in 2nd Kings 6:17, where Elisha prayed for God to open the sight of his young attendant, and immediately the young man saw the chariots of fire. But in Rev. 6:9–11, these souls under the altar (Tribulation Saints) ask how long, O Lord? But God tells them to wait until their brothers a slain as they were slain (beheaded). But what if the answer is NO. It appears that this parable of the persistent widow fits into this answer. But???????

Sidebar notes

Here we know God cannot be cajoled, but her (and our) continual prayer request for God to continue motivating the person (in this case, the Judge) to do the right thing (justice) eventually. Here is proof we are *to continue to pray for those lost individuals, at present, who do not want to hear about Jesus' salvation.* The Judge's answer could be any of the three, but you and I are not aware of God's future plans for that individual's life. In Rom. 9, we read of the potter and the clay.

Romans 9:21–23 *"(21) Hath not the potter power over the clay, of the same lump to make one vessel unto honour, and another unto dishonour? (22)* **What if God, willing to shew his wrath, and to make his power known, endured with much longsuffering the vessels of wrath fitted to destruction:** *(23) And that he might make known the riches of his glory on the vessels of mercy, which he had afore prepared unto glory."*

These words should humble us to understand that we are not fully aware of God's intimate plan for all humans he created and what God has in store for the different souls on earth.

What if someone had killed Paul for persecuting the early Christian Jews? God created Paul for his missionary efforts and to write all his letters for us today. Many criminals have converted to Jesus and been very productive in saving souls in prisons.

We, at present, do not have the complete mind of Christ. But when we are made incorruptible, we will be given the mind of Jesus. Only then will we be the perfect Judge. But, as humans, we are to depend on God's perfect word for our evaluation in judgments.

Verse 8 is best clarified by knowing the future prophecies in the Bible. Here is a short, to the point, review for your consideration:

1. We are saved by faith alone.
2. Treasures come from the deeds (works) we have performed.
3. The Rapture treasure is from faith and deeds. (Sheep)

The Great Tribulation

4. The Tribulation Saints have faith (goats), no deeds, therefore, no treasures.
5. The Tribulation Saints must perform deeds (works) of refusing the Mark of the Beast and more. (Thereby, becoming Wheat)
6. The dead Tribulation Saints will be housed under the Altar in Heaven. Both the dead Old Testament Saints and dead Tribulation Saints will be harvested in the 1st Harvest.
7. Many of the converted Jews and gentiles will survive the Great Tribulation and go into the 1,000-year-Kingdom of Jesus.

Therefore, Jesus will find faith on earth by the survivors and converts saved by their faith conversion during the 144,000 missionaries (Rev.7). These verses of scripture should reveal to us the linage of injustice. It will be present for all ages to experience and not be surprised by human perpetuations of injustice in high places, manipulated by Machiavellian, greedy, insistent, ruthless individuals.

This *unrighteous widow* used a non-religious concept to meet her wants. And she could care less about the injustice she may be inflicting on the other person. Vengeance is hated, and God wants us to love and be charitable to our enemies. So much for love, your neighbor!

The *righteous widow* is recognizing that injustice is happening every day. She will not forget this injustice, but attempt, through non-violent prayers, to change injustice to justice. This concept should be the Christian's force for change. It is not sinning to try to insist on truth for an event that has happened to Christians. We are to fight against injustice. But God wants you to know he is in control; nothing will happen to you that God does not permit. He wants us to be wrapped in peace in our hearts with this faith that passes all understanding. But the fight for right, Justice, and Jesus' ways is a Christian's duty.

Abortions (murders) are one of the hideous crimes against unprotected innocent babies. These babies had nothing to do with the lust of the flesh committed by the mother or the rape of the mother. The babies' right to life, liberty, and the pursuit of happiness has been stolen from them. Birth is a natural event created by God. And the death of the mother is now an extremely low possibility. If complications occur, a C section can be performed to eliminate this threat for her and, in most cases, also save the baby.

In Jesus 1,000 Kingdom, both the mother and the perpetrator of abortion will both be killed for murder, and they will not go to heaven (1st John 3:15) but the Lake of Fire. However, there is NO SIN that cannot be forgiven by God, except ***Blaspheming the Holy Spirit.***

Christians <u>are not</u> the Kinsman Redeemers YET, for we have not the mind of Christ YET. So, our prayers are our best and most powerful tool against evil principalities or powers. However, prayer does not eliminate our physical responsibility to act righteously during periods of harmful unrighteous behavior. Vengeance and violence are generally not Christians' answers to evil, but it can become necessary to destroy evil (World War II and Armageddon). Continue praying in the hope of a soon answer of YES. Even God will approve of violence during War#1 of Armageddon and War #2 of Rev.20:7–11. God is revealing to us the only way to remove evil; is to kill it. *But remember, only God knows who is evil and whether they will change to righteousness in the future.*

"How think ye?" now.

If you want to see the corrupted attitude prophecy revealing this is coming in magnitude, go to 2nd Tim. 3.

2nd Timothy 3:1–5 *"(1) **This also know that in the last days perilous <u>times</u>** shall come. (2) **For men shall be lovers of their own selves, covetous, boasters, proud, blasphemers, disobedient to parents, unthankful, unholy, (3) Without natural affection, trucebreakers, false accusers, incontinent, fierce, despisers of those that are good, (4) Traitors, heady, highminded, lovers of pleasures more than lovers of God; (5) <u>Having a form</u>** of godliness, but denying the power thereof: from such turn away.</u> (6) **For of this sort are they which creep into houses, and lead captive silly women laden with sins, led away with divers lusts, (7) Ever learning, and never able to come to the knowledge of the truth. (8) Now as Jannes and Jambres withstood Moses, so do these also resist the truth: men of corrupt minds, reprobate concerning the faith. (9) But they shall proceed no further: <u>for their folly shall be manifest unto all</u>** men**, as theirs also was."*

Some of these traits have been seen in years past, but not everyone on this list is found here. The <u>clue</u> here is in verse 5. There it speaks of religious leaders, *"having the form (look) of Godliness, but denying the power thereof."* Open your eyes and see all of these being fulfilled today. Homosexual churches, homosexual Pastors, strange offshoots (James Jones, etc.), Priest sexually abusing children, Bishops lying and the hiding of priest abusers, injustice for those children by clergy, the law punishment of child abuse not upheld, abortion is child abuse, and on and on. Awake, my friends and brothers; *times are a-changing for evil!*

LESSONS LEARN

At Least

1. Remember, Jurisprudence. *Innocence until proven guilty without a shadow of a doubt.*
2. Do not initially make assumptions based on: traditions, little evidence, or gossip (news media).
3. Do not be affected by either side's rank in the social position.
4. First, listen intently, makes notes, Ask questions for clarity.
5. Look for discrepancies.
6. Study the case for clues.
7. Find answers to these clues.
8. Determine the validity of clue connections.
9. Know the law about this type of case.
10. Know both individuals' character and record.
11. Let no outside unverified information influence the verdict—news articles without a witness to verify and especially rumors.
12. Verify all facts are supported by God's Words, the Bible.
13. Determine the just outcome needed, be it not guilty or guilty.
14. Use God's word as to the punishment God finds correct.

JUDGMENT

The verdict must be on the truth. Also, the conclusion must be based on God's law and man's law. Jesus or God will judge us all based on God's justification of punishment for that crime listed in the Bible. *Infidelity has a death sentence by God.* A death sentence for those two is ---- God's justice, not the judges. The judge is only repeating God's judgment. Only when the Judge's punishment is less than or more than God's quoted punishment, or when the Judge invents a Law, is when the Judge is judging. Remember, Christians and Tribulation Saints, only, will be judges in Jesus' Kingdom. But, keep in mind mercy, if at all possible.

We read in Mat.6:14 a requirement for us before exercising the law.

Matthew 6:14–15 *"(14) For if ye forgive men their trespasses, your heavenly Father will also forgive you: (15) But if ye forgive not men their trespasses, neither will your Father forgive your trespasses."*

Here *appears* a contradictory statement by Jesus. 1) How can we judge with God's laws without the punishment to which God tells us about his just punishment for that sin? And 2) how can we judge if we forgive all sinful actions? Does this not appear as a dichotomy? We are not looking at this correctly *but on an assumption of traditions.* In our traditions, we are to forgive all sins which ignore God's laws. But there are two considerations for us. Which is the most egregious, Mortal Sin or Eternal Sin?

Mortal Sin is those sins committed against us while we are alive on this earth. This is the sin we are to judge under God's laws. Even Jesus on the cross did not pray for the thief to be removed (forgiven from his mortal death); because it was just punishment by Roman Law. But *Jesus asks God to forgive the thief on the cross his <u>eternal spiritual death</u> and later revealed God honored Jesus' request (thief would be in Paradise). <u>Jesus did not pray to remove that thief's just earthly punishment</u>.* The proof is provided by the thief's death on the cross, but in Paradise with Jesus.

You will also notice in Jesus' death on the Cross, Jesus prayed to God to forgive the perpetrators for his death; *"Father forgive them for they know not what they do."* Jesus is praying for forgiveness for their eternal death. *"How think ye?"*

We should recognize our sins here on earth; it is one way God will chastise us for our disobedience. This chastisement is God's way to reinforce the need for us to be obedient. If we forgive them and remove God's chastisement, they will not learn the lesson God desires for them. We are told that we will judge them in Jesus' 1,000-year Kingdom for their earthly disobedience.

We also will be judged by the Books, and one is the Bible. It reveals sin and punishment for that sin. If we use the Bible in Judging, we are not judging but repeating God's Judgments for that sin.

And we (Christians) will be judged by Jesus, but the lost by God. So, we see 2 Judgments, mortal (earthly) and spiritual (eternal), for crimes and sins.

Being we are earthly; our forgiveness request is for *Eternal Judgment.* However, we too must forgive and house no anger, and *we must ask God to forgive their eternal sin but not necessarily their earthly sin.* To forgive a sin against us is for our benefit of peace in our hearts, but for us to seek earthy accountability of that sin is proper. Without justice and payment of that justice, our world will become like the Days of Noah, anarchy, requiring the same judgment of total death destruction again. This event is proven in scriptures by War #1 and War #2. Evil must be destroyed, but only God knows who is evil or will later accept Jesus and be forgiven. We do not have this knowledge yet.

Jesus himself will not let sinners into his city, Jerusalem, during the 1,000-years Kingdom. Nor will God into his city of Rev. 21:24–27.

Do not jump to conclusions without more in-depth consideration. Rumors are the most prevalent today, and we *Christians are not to participate in rumors.* Another plentiful sin here is lying. Christians have accepted this sin in their everyday life without consideration.

Just because a respectable person says they have evidence of a crime, *it is a worthless statement.* If they had proof, they would have presented it for verification for truth; then and only then can it be accepted as fact. Lies abound even after swearing to give *"the truth and nothing but the truth."* Lying under oath is very seldom charged against a person, so why not lie. Well, God hates lies, even little white lies or exaggerations, for they are not the truth.

With all this said, remember Jesus words in 1ˢᵗ Pet.4:8.

1ˢᵗ Peter 4:8, *"And above all things have fervent charity among yourselves: for charity shall cover the multitude of sins."*

In many Bibles, Charity is labeled LOVE, the definition in Greek means:

15. **"ag-ap-oh'-o;** perh. from *äyar agan* (*much*) [or 5689]; to love (in a social or moral sense): –(be-) love (-ed). Comp.5368 speaks of tenderness and to *kiss* (mark of tenderness)[1]."

Not to be confused with:

16. **"ag-ah'-pay**: from 25; love, i.e., affection or benevolence; spec. (plur.) a love feast: – (feast of) charity ([-ably)], dear, love[1]."

As you can see, both words appear to go together. **25** speaks of much social or moral sense of love. This type of love seems more brotherly love. The kiss was a friendly jester when meeting.

26 speaks of a love feast (also from 25) and affection or benevolence and a love feast. If we combine, these two we get a brotherly love feast. Does this not have the all-encompassing Love of God.

God created us with the emotion of hate and then requires us to control that emotion. I find it difficult to understand how we could love Satan or anyone who has killed a loved one. We are not capable of getting that warm fussy loving feeling for that person. However, we can be charitable.

In 1ˢᵗ Cor. 5, we are *told not to judge* those outsides of the Church but those inside the Church. For those outside the Church, God will judge. One thing about judging is, judging carries with it a guilty or innocent result and its repercussions. However, those outside the Church can be evaluated as good or evil, but no judgments. Right?

Just the opposite. These are the people we are to go to and share the gospel within the hope of bringing Jesus' salvation into their life. But to recognize the lost souls, we must be able to evaluate them as needing Jesus.

Before correcting a brother in Christ, make sure that working in this situation is not one of your serious temptations you battle.

1ˢᵗ Corinthians 5:12–13 *"For what have I to do to judge them also that are without? do not <u>ye judge them that are within? (13) But them that are <u>without God judgeth. Therefore, put away from among yourselves that wicked person.</u>"*

But while on this earth, we have guidelines before judging a person inside the Church. But continue in prayer for this person during this time.

Galatians 6:1 *"(1) Brethren, if a man be overtaken in a fault, ye which are spiritual, restore such an one in the spirit of meekness; <u>considering thyself, lest thou also be tempted.</u>"*

Here God is telling us to look first inside our life's weaknesses. If you are battling the same particular weakness in your life, remain clear of this individual. But you might find a spiritual spokesperson for him. If it is not a temptation for you, then have confidence in the next scripture.

2ⁿᵈ Timothy 3:16–17 *"(16) All scripture* is given by inspiration of God, and is <u>profitable for doctrine, for reproof, for correction, for instruction in righteousness: (17) That the man of God may be perfect, throughly furnished unto all good works.</u>"*

Pray for this situation before you get involved. Let the Holy Spirit guide you in scripture preparation before going to this person. Remember to present your petition in love and kindness one on one. We see this one on one in Mat.18

Matthew 18:15–17 *"(15) Moreover if thy brother shall trespass against thee, go and tell him his fault <u>between thee and him alone:</u> if he shall hear thee, thou hast gained thy brother. (16) But if he will not hear thee, <u>then take with thee one or two more,</u> that in the mouth of two or three witnesses every word may be established. (17) And if <u>he shall neglect to</u> <u>hear them,</u> <u>tell</u> it <u>unto the church:</u> but if he neglect to hear the church, let him be unto thee as an <u>heathen man and a publican.</u>"*

<u>Verse 15 </u>is clear that we must go one on one with the person that has offended us. This action shows respect and protects his reputation. This action is also a fair business practice. Never embarrass someone in public as you have set the stage for anger and opposition. I must share one caveat if it is a man and a woman, with the woman, take another trustworthy woman with you but keep her as visual but outside of hearing distance.

<u>Verse 16</u>, But if the opposition is the initial results, then find at least one other person to go with you again to the person to establish a witness of that person's rejection of your rightful petition. And if he still rejects the righteous appeal, this rejecter must be brought before the Church. And if there is still no change, then this man is to be put out of the Church. Notice this says to bring this person before the Church, not just the elders.

Today the Church elders are considered the Church, but; this is not what the Bible says. If it is not the Church, how is the Church to know not to eat with this rejecter? We see this requirement in 1st Cor. 5:11.

1st Corinthians 5:11 *"But now I have written unto you not to keep company, if any man that is called a brother be a fornicator, or covetous, or an idolater, or a railer, or a drunkard, or an extortioner; with an one do not to eat."*

This verse of scripture reveals the Communion of the bread and wine. The only way to prevent this is to remove this person from the Church. 1st Cor. 5 supports this concept:8–13.

1st Corinthians 5:8 *"(8) Therefore let us <u>keep the feast</u> [communion], <u>not with old leaven</u>, neither <u>with the leaven of malice and wickedness;</u> but with <u>the unleavened</u> bread of sincerity <u>and truth</u>. (13) But them that are without God judgeth. Therefore, put away from among yourselves that wicked person."*

Even though the Church rejects the rejecter, this does not mean we should forget him or her. He or she is still a child of God who needs prayer and instructions.

**Hopefully, this instruction could be done
before his rejection from the Church.**

CAUTION

This situation has caused many Churches to split. This splitting is especially true if the rejecter is an extremely popular person. And/or the process has been performed incorrectly. It is essential to have correct proof and not a word-of-mouth gossip. Present the rejection to the Church in such a way to minimize questions but allow questions. Do not lose your temper and get confrontational. If they do not want to understand, they will not be able to understand and are only supported by their friends.

I like these words of verses of scripture that says:

James 1:19–20 *"Wherefore, my beloved brethren, let every man <u>be swift to hear</u>, <u>slow to speak</u>, <u>slow to wrath</u>: (20) For the wrath of man worketh not the righteousness of God."*

CHAPTER 7

Pharisee and Tax Collector

Luke 18:9—14 *"(9) And he [Jesus] spake this <u>parable unto certain which trusted in themselves that they were righteous, and despised others:</u> (10) Two men went up into the temple to pray; the one a Pharisee, and the other a publican. (11) The Pharisee stood and prayed thus with himself, God, I thank thee, that I am not as other men are, extortioners, unjust, adulterers, or even as this publican. (12) I fast twice in the week, I give tithes of all that I possess. (13) And the publican, standing afar off, would not lift up so much as his eyes unto heaven, but smote upon his breast, saying, God be merciful to me a sinner me a sinner. (14) I tell you, this man went down to his <u>house</u> justified rather than the other: for every one that exalteth himself shall be <u>abased</u>; and he that humbleth himself shall be exalted."*

The *1ˢᵗ clue* found here is in verse 9. The first part of the sentence of *trusting in themselves and despised others* reveals they believe their works justifies them to God above others. PRIDE! They believed in obeying the law was their way to salvation. And at that time, was the truth taught to them by the Priest and Rabbis. This perfection was precise, but it was not completely understood that it pointed to the *perfection of Jesus.* They did not also recognize that they should only trust in God and not in themselves. They failed to realize that the law pertained to their hearts as well as their outward actions. The Pharisees did the deeds required (tithes) but missed the point of their heart. They were taught of Abraham's faith in God to perform Isaac's sacrifice attempt and for God to keep his covenant with Abraham. Isaac must survive to provide children, such as the *sands of the sea.*

Here is a revealing to Christians our trust is in Jesus (God) and not in our idea of righteousness. Deeds were and will always be required from Adam to the end of time. But Abraham revealed the companion to deeds for salvation, but FAITH now takes precedence over deeds. Jesus also promoted this concept, which was not well accepted. Jesus taught deeds are for treasures, and faith replaced deeds for salvation.

Another *clue* is also in Verse 9, "*and they despised others.*" This attitude is from the heart of this Pharisee. *Others* include other people who they felt were below the Pharisee's righteousness, *sinners.* The Pharisee was prideful and judgmental of this Tax collector, which most people hated. They ignored Jesus' teaching of "*Love your enemies*" and "*do good to them that hate you.*"

Verse 10 reveals the location of this event, which is at the Temple of God on earth. The Pharisee is in the Temple, while the publican stood far away from the Pharisee.

Note

There are two groups mentioned in the Bible, which are the Pharisee and Sadducee. The differences between the two are:

1. Pharisees = gave equal credit to traditions as they did to the Torah (Book of Law). They believed in the resurrection of the dead. They developed the Mishnah that referred to the continuance of Judaism after the destruction of the Temple. And this concept *formed Rabbinic Judaism today.* They also were less motivated by the politics of the day. They believed in the afterlife and the spiritual world of angels and demons.

2. Sadducees = were more politically motivated aristocratic elitist and more wealthy. Being political, they held more powerful jobs in the government and religion. Sadducees did not believe in the resurrection of the dead. They also were more accommodating to the Romans than were the Pharisees. The Sadducees did not believe in the afterlife or the spiritual world of angels or demons. Sadducees did not trust traditions; if it was not in the scriptures (Tanakh), it was not valid.

3. Most of the Court was filled with both Pharisees and Sadducees. However. After the dispersion in 70 ADS, the Sadducees ceased to exist.

In <u>verses 11–12,</u> the clarity of this Pharisee's heart comes into Jesus' light. The Pharisee brags on himself to God, who knows his faults. He has no concept of the sins he has committed in his heart. God wants us to love fellow sinners, reveal God's love for them. We are not to judge lost but only those within the Church. As humans, we are subject to pride in self accomplishments without the understanding that it is God who provided us the talent and opportunity to succeed. There appears to be no humility in this Pharisee's heart. But notice the stark difference between the Pharisee heart and the publican's (Tax collector) heart.

<u>Verse 13</u> The publican stood far off, feeling unworthy to enter God's Temple. He is so ashamed of his sins that he does not look up to God in heaven. He also recognizes he is a sinner and is remorseful and *repenting for his sins*. The publican is hoping for God's grace to forgive him and be merciful to his soul. But verse 14 makes a possible overlooked statement.

<u>In verse 14</u>, both Pharisee and the publican go home (*house*). House is a metaphor for our house in eternity. Because Jesus has not come yet in this historical parable, the law was the Hebrew's primary deed required to perform. In their attempt to keep the law, God's mercy was added to deeds for salvation. Both these men will go to the *house* God

has prepared for them, be it Heaven or Lake of Fire. *Those who exalt themselves will be abased, but the humbled will be exalted.*

The word **abased** = "*To lower in position, rank, prestige, or estimation; cast down; humble.*"

For those individuals, who have deceived themselves about their valued status in Jesus and God's Kingdom, they will be abased. Cast down in prestige and from a higher position to be humbled.

"5013 = **tap-i-nŏ'-o:** from *5011*; to *depress*: fig. to *humiliate* (in condition or heart): --abase, bring low, humble (self)[1]."

This concept may need some explaining, I think! Let us return to the house mentioned in verse 14. Jesus tells us that he is building a mansion for our eternal home (1st John 14:2–3). This house appears to be for Christians. What of the great men of the Bible like Enoch, Elijah, Moses, Abram, Mary, the apostles, and others? They, too, also deserve a mansion. *But this is the potter's choice.* However, there is no doubt for Christians. Christians are told we will be kings, lords, and priests (1st Timothy 6:15 and Rev.1:6). Therefore, let us look into the religious government of Jesus' reign on earth.

In Rev.19: 16, the return of Jesus to conquer the earth, and his name is *"KING OF KINGS AND LORD OF LORDS."* But coming with him is the Church, the Bride of Christ; we will be kings and lords below the KING of kings and LORD of Lords. God places Jesus singularly as the ultimate KING above all other kings. If Christians are kings, who are the king's over? In Rev. 15:4, the word reveals that all nations shall come and worship before Jesus. Therefore, we must be kings of and in these nations. All nations may speak the same language then. If all the nations present in from the universe, we would need a common language between all languages. God first created us with a universal language in the beginning. Now Jesus gives us the organizational structure of

Jesus' righteous Kingdom. His Kingdom will be a monarchy with Jesus as its king. Then Jesus may select certain Saints to be the major kings of those nations and just under Jesus' leadership. Also, there could be minor kings chosen to rule a county or providence and to rule under the major king of nations. Even so, we see lords in which might be the Major of a city and a village. Priests should be assigned to each ruler and be the teacher to the survivors and their children.

*See next page for the possible simplistic organizational structure of Jesus' government, **and it is only an assumption on my part.***

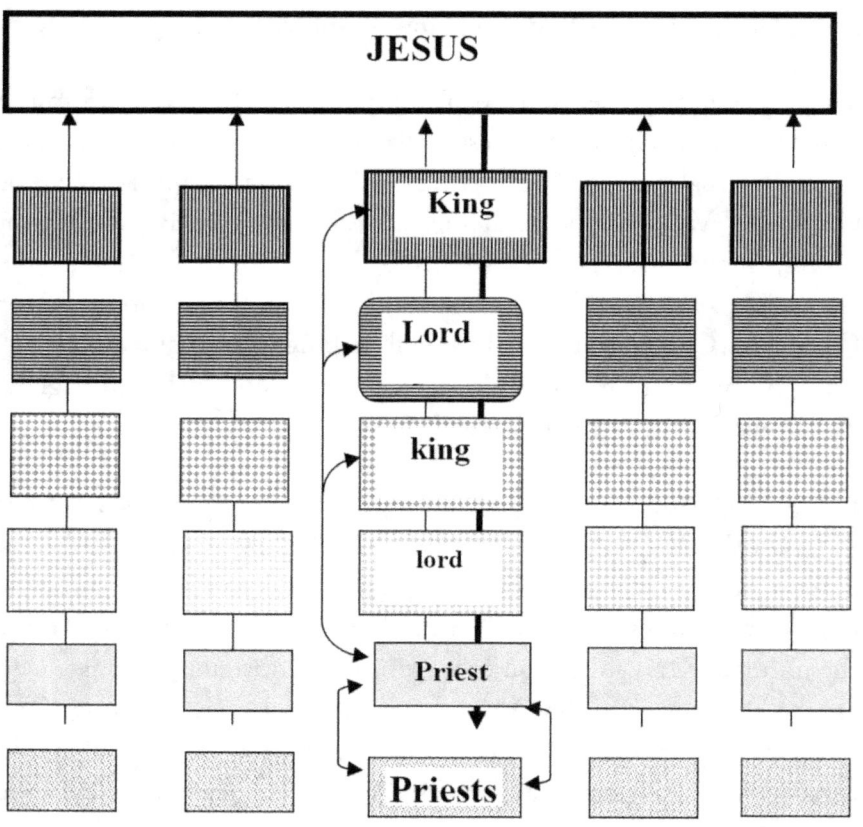

4. The **King of a Nation** = A king for each nation of Jesus' design on the earth. *Example: America.*

5. The **King of a State** = lesser king like a governor and responsible to the King of that Nation. *Example: Tennessee.*

6. The **Lord of a County** = is like our County Mayor but accountable to the King of the State. Example: *Knox County*

7. The **lord of a City** = is like our City Mayor responsible to the County Major. Example: *Knoxville Major.*

8. The **Priest** = is the religious group of counselors to the kings or lords to whom they are assigned. They also are responsible for civilians for teaching.

9. Survivors and children = are the survivors (of the Great Tribulation) and their children born during the 1,000-years of Jesus' Kingdom. Many of these children will be part of Satan's army after the 1,000 years whom God will destroy.

1. ***All the above will be under Jesus (King of kings and Lord of lords') leadership during his 1,000- year Kingdom.***

The Law of the land will be the law revealed in the Bible (Torah). Jesus proves this law in his statement shown in Mat. 5.

Matthew 5:18, "For verily I say unto you, Till heaven and earth pass, one jot or one tittle shall in no wise pass from the law, till all be fulfilled."

This verse clarifies that the Torah's law will be used in Jesus' Kingdom until War #2 by God against Satan and his army, which is completely destroyed, and then God creates the New Heaven and New Earth.

LESSONS LEARNED

1. The Beatitudes of Mathew chapters 5, 6, and 7 reveal the attitudes we are to have for our fellow man.

2. No matter a person's status in this life, we all are sinners worthy of death. We all are failures (sinners) in this life, and it is God who gives us the abilities and opportunities to succeed better than others. Our pride should be in what God has done for us and not what we think we only have achieved by our labors.

3. God gives, and God takes away. Remember Samson's story. He was powerful until he sinned against God, and God removed his strength. Also, David's sin with Bathsheba was punishment by his son's death, whom he loved immensely.

4. There are global repercussions for turning against God. Israel suffered many times for worshipping other gods during their history.

5. Revelation's book reveals the global upheavals that will occur, showing God's displeasure and the approaching time of the end, which most earthlings will ignore.

6. Without humility, we will think better of ourselves. And therefore deceive ourselves by opening the door of our hearts to sin.

CHAPTER 8

The Unmerciful Servant

Matthew 18:23–32 "(23) <u>Therefore</u> is the kingdom of heaven likened unto a certain king, which would take <u>account</u> of his servants. (24)And when he had begun to reckon, one was brought unto him, <u>which owed him ten thousand talents.</u> (25) <u>But forasmuch as he had not to pay, his lord commanded him to be sold, and his wife, and children, and all that he had, and payment to be made.</u> (26) The servant therefore fell, and worshipped him, saying, Lord, have patience with me, and I will pay thee all. (27) Then the lord of that servant was moved with <u>compassion, and loosed him, and forgave him the debt.</u> (28) But the <u>same servant went out</u> and found one of his fellowservants, which owed him an hundred pence: and he laid hands on him, and took him by the throat, saying, Pay me that thou owest. (29) And <u>his fellowservant fell down at his feet, and besought him, saying, Have patience with me, and I will pay thee all.</u> (30) And he would not: but <u>went and cast him into prison,</u> till he should pay the <u>debt.</u> (31) So when his fellowservants saw what was done, they were very sorry, and came and told unto their lord all that was done. (32) <u>Then his lord, after that he had called him,</u> said unto him, O thou wicked servant, <u>I forgave thee all that debt,</u> because thou desiredst me: (33) <u>Shouldest not thou also have had compassion on thy fellowservant, even as I had pity on thee?</u> (34) And his lord was wroth, and delivered him to the tormentors, till he should pay all that was due unto him. (35) So

likewise shall my heavenly Father do also unto you, <u>if ye from your</u> <u>hearts forgive not every one his brother their trespasses.</u>"

Before you study these verses, please return to the beginning of Chapter 18, and read to verse 23, as the attitudes and information run hand in hand. There you will read of:

1. Ambitions of the disciples are rebuked. (Not apostils) Mat. 18:1–6.
2. The Stumbling-blocks warning. (Mat. 18:7–10)
3. The Lost Sheep. (Mat.18:11–14)
4. Discipline Procedures for Dissident Brother. (Mat. 18:15–19)
5. Unlimited forgiveness. (Mat. 18:19–22)
6. Our duty to be Merciful. (Mat.18:27–35)

Notice these parables emphasis' is based on earth and our life's experiences on earth. If a parable is designed to take known knowledge to unknown spiritual knowledge, then we must first be taught the earthly knowledge. So, in Chapter 18, God reveals to us the worldly knowledge first and then our actions.

Note

The verses of scripture that the Catholics believe introduces the place they call Purgatory. Purgatory in the Catholic doctrine is the location where unforgiven sinners go after death to pay for their sins. This concept appears erroneous, as the Bible says after death comes judgment. Jesus' mission on earth was to pay for all sins. Jesus made the complete payment, not us. How long would it take to pay for sin? Nowhere in the Bible is there a time measurement for payment for different sins.

In <u>verse 23</u>, we read of the king's desire to take an account of his servants' deeds. This account is a one-time event to judge his servant's deeds and results. This accounting also can spiritually represent a one-time event in Judgment. We in Christ will be judged by Christ (Judgment Seat of Christ) and the judgment of all lost souls (The Great White Throne Judgment of God). There will be different events at various times. The following words give us not only the sin but also the judgment for that particular sin.

Also, keep in mind that we are being judged continuously by Jesus and God for our actions and attitudes. The Book of Remembrances is God's daily diary of every individual on earth. And this Record of Account will be used, opened to reveal every action, word, and evil thought we have done in our lifetime.

In verse 24, the king begins with his *first servant*. Notice this is the servant of God! I am not sure about his choice to call first, be it alphabetical, oldest or youngest. I would think Adam would be first. But if it is for the lost, Cain might be first as this is God's Great White Thorne Judgment (the lost).

This servant owed the king 10 thousand talents; in today's money, it is an extreme amount, which the servant could not payback.

Verse 25 reveals the just punish of this man. Therefore, this servant falls under the Law of Mosses must sell all that man owns to pay his debt, including his wife and children. For us today, this is not acceptable. But it is to God, and he is trying to impress man, even up to today, the seriousness of debt. God gives us freedom from our debt of sin. But, if we have not attempted to return value for Jesus' death for us, we will have to give up all we possess. How can this be revealed in spiritual terms?

Remember, *we owe Jesus for our eternal life, for he paid our debt of sins.* So, we have a tremendous obligation due. Our debt payment is in our service deeds. Without deeds (attempt to pay back), those will need to sell all they own. Can this be the spiritual equivalent of missing the Rapture? Those Christians who have paid their obligation are Raptured, and those ½ christians who have not will lose all they own and need to start the work to fulfill their obligation. This fulfillment plan will be challenging, and many will fail (fall away).

Verse 26 is fascinating as it reveals a new fulfillment plan from God. The servant is distraught and realizes he has sinned against the Lord. Notice the Lord is used to identify the king. Jesus, who has paid that servant's sin debt and He is moved by the servant's repentant heart. Hopefully, this represents the attitude of most of the left behind ½ christians. Now they are asking forgiveness for their lack of deeds. And are willing to fulfill with an act of rejecting Satan's Mark of the Beast. Thereby, many of these Tribulation Saints will be beheaded.

In verse 27, we see the lord is moved by his servant's repentance, shows mercy, and removes all debts (salvation).

But now, this servant reverts to his old ways.

Verse 28–29 reveals this forgiven servant reverts to his old ways. This servant now goes to one of his fellow-servants who owed him 100 pence (much less than his debit). And he abused him by taking him by the throat, threatening to punish him unless he was paid. But the fellow-servant made the same request but to no avail.

In verse 30, the fellow servant was cast into jail by the first servant until all the debt was paid. Do you see the same situation but a different outcome? This verse reveals the future actions the Tribulation Saints can expect in those left behind who becomes Satan's cronies (fallen away).

But in verses 31, that evil servant is revealed by either angels or those dead Tribulation Saints held under the Temple Altar in Heaven.

Not sure why this is inserted here, as God knows everything that is happening. Therefore, it must be for our use.

Verse 32–33, we see the final result for this evil servant of God. His actions are leading to the Great White Throne Judgment of God. He is brought to God, who judges him by revealing his past and present continued sins.

In verse 34, God is terribly angry and casts him to the tormentors until his debt is fully paid. What do you think the payment will be for unrepentant sinners or those who have blasphemed the Holy Spirit? *Payment will never be fulfilled.*

These are the left behind who fall away from Jesus and God to worship Satan. After they die, they are cast into Hell (Tormentors) *with other lost souls already there, and Hell is eventually cast into the Lake of Fire forever.* (Rev. 20:14)

Verse 35 is an extreme warning to you and me. If Jesus forgave us our **eternal** sin against God, likewise, we must also forgive our brothers for their **eternal** sins against us.

Matthew 6:14–15 *"(14) For if ye forgive men their trespasses, your heavenly Father will also forgive you: (15) But if ye forgive not men their trespasses, neither will your Father forgive your trespasses".*

We have looked into this forgiveness before, and it is clear this forgiveness is for eternal judgment. Hatred and anger against another person or persons are devastating to the victim's life if he does not forgive the perpetrator against him. The constant mental aggregation is known to affect the victim's health. And it will also affect those around the victim and cause them problems too. Forgive, live in peace, and pray for those who have abused you or those you love. Seek earthly justice, if necessary, but remember to show mercy in Judgment.

LESSONS LEARNED

1. We are to be considered servants of Jesus and God.
2. As servants, we must visually act and physically perform deeds required by the will of our Master, Jesus.
3. Our physical action should reflect the righteousness of Jesus. There must not be even the appearance of improper actions on our part.
4. We must love and forgive and help those in need; we must think of them more highly than we of ourselves.
5. We are not to speak ill of no one or to spread gossip. Watch out, as this one can be performed in a prayer request.
6. We are to think positively rather than negatively.
7. We should give credit where credit is due.
8. If we see a need for righteousness, we are to fulfill that need. If we do not, then that is the sin of omission.
9. We must do to others as we would like them to do for us.
10. Remember, what goes around, comes around.
11. Treat people better than you have been treated.
12. Be charitable to your enemy.
13. Deal honestly with others; no cheating; it is stealing.
14. Repay debts quickly.
15. Lend to brothers without interest

CHAPTER 9

New cloth sewed onto an old cloth

Matthew 9:16–17 *"No man putteth a piece of new cloth unto an old garment, for that which is put in to fill it up taketh from the garment, and the rent is made worse. (17) Neither do men put new wine into old bottles: else the bottles break, and the wine runneth out, and the bottles perish: but they put new wine into new bottles, and both are preserved."*

This parable appears a straightforward parable to understand. It is short and sweet and known by most people. Remember Jesus is using a known concept to the spiritual concept. Most people know that new cloth shrinks more than old cloth, as it has shrunk about all it will shrink. Therefore, the old material will not match the new fabric's shrinkage and become severely deformed cloth, or if the fabric is secured on all sides, the new will shrink so much it will rip out the old material.

Jesus is referring to his new gospel of saved by faith.

The Hebrew people have been living under the Law of Moses for many years. It has been ingrained into them by Moses and the following Priest, Rabbis, fathers for over a thousand years. Moses received the 10 Commandments in circa 1440 BC, and Jesus' mission started in circa 0025 AD. The Law of Moses has so much volume; it had to be ingrained into the people. It also gave much power to the Priest.

An individual who broke the law was punished quickly by the people's hands and not the Priest. Everyone in the village was to watch or participate in their punishment, not like today. We have become so soft-hearted that seeing God's righteous punishment appears far worse than the crime. Not seeing the punishment removes the stigma of seeing a person in agronomy and removes any effects not to do what that person did. No one is stoned to death by God's Law today. A few people attend the chemical death of an individual, and they are affected by that death. But there are few who attend these events.

It was in this environment Jesus came to teach an opposing doctrine. The majority knew what was right, and it had worked perfectly for over a thousand years. They were comfortable in their spiritual life. They did not believe they had to be perfect in the law to be with God in eternity. God and Jesus, on the other hand, were knowledgeable of the hereafter and the many lost souls. Here we also see the concept of, *"we haven't done that way in the past."* Learning what God wanted them to know had been eliminated.

Jesus came to earth in this corrupt environment to bring salvation and knowledge to the lost. The spiritual leaders hated him as Jesus' concepts diametrically opposed the Priest and Rabbis'. Their inability to accept new knowledge was their downfall. We see this attitude in our Churches today. Keep the sermon and lessons sweet, loving, positive, and not new truths, challenging, and non-confrontational (Itchy ear).

We see a second attempt to limiting the truthful education for the masses, which came through the 1st Christian Church. The beginning of the Church was small groups that gather to learn about Jesus and salvation. And then they would go out to the people to tell them about Jesus. Today we have changed this procedure to; bring the people into the Church so the pastor can save them. (Wrong and Right). But the pastor is not your scapegoat. This idea was new to the Hebrews as they were never required to go to people and tell them about the one and only God. This lack of effort was so ingrained into them that even today, they stay isolated. No missionaries to the gentiles.

Today our Churches have become like the Church of Laodicea. Money is the prime consideration (internal). Many Churches have accumulated such a debt that the debt is unpayable when old money dies off. I can assure you; this is not what God wants for his children.

This old garment mentioned here in this parable was the Hebrews that came to existence during the Law period. The new cloth is the new doctrine Jesus brought with him. This new system will have troubles as the shrinkage comes with the new doctrine to pull apart the old doctrine. This old cloth is tearing apart the old Jewish ways. They have the traditional Jews, the progressive Jews, and the non-Jewish Jew. Old habits are hard to break. However, the 144,000 Jewish Missionaries **(Rev.7)** will bring the Jews to Jesus during the Great Tribulation.

This tribulation is the period of proof to Israel that Jesus is their Messiah. The events will be clear to the Jewish people and their leaders, that the prophecies of the Old Testament and new Testament agree. However, if they are not knowable of the Book of Revelation, how will they be able to compare. For my Christian friends, Israel is God's chosen people. We are to go to them, too.

We need to share the gospel with them, remember they have been blinded by God and God has commanded us to reveal the truth, in love, to our soon to be brother and sisters in Christ. But how do we do that? The fog of false doctrine, and traditions, are so thick between Christians and Jews, it by itself, will be difficult to clear up. It is my hope, and prayer, that this book will be and open door for both Jew and gentile to know Jesus' gospel is true.

I am sorry to say, the motivation will not be inspired until after the Rapture event and the prophetic consequences of the Great Tribulation of seven years. Pain is the only way to inspire some people. Hopefully, we Christians can be the start for inspiration of the 144,000 Jewish Missionaries to Israel.

They will need some knowledge of their history, old law, new law, Jesus Messiahship, future events, prophecies completed, prophesies yet to come, and salvation from the Lake of Fire.

Christians can you not feel the desperation of those who experience being left behind. The separation from the love they unknowing had, like Jesus' death on the cross." E'lĭ, E'lĭ, lā'mȧ sȧ-băch'-tha-nĭ. "

"My God, My God, why hast thou forsaken Me."

His broken heart-----to heal our hearts.

Only those who have experienced this feeling of abandonment will know the internal feeling of pain of the heart. The absolute depth of depression and the desire to remove that pain. And knowing that pain will never end.

As teenagers going through our internal chemical change of puberty, and your sweetheart affections changed for another person, you may remember the that feeling of abandonment and that it will never end, and life was not worth living.

This is a scratch on the surface compared to Jesus' heart break. This is a surprise to Jesus, for his obedience to die and pay for all individuals total sins. This statement made by Jesus may reveal the abandonment feeling of great magnitude. So great, it may be what actually killed Jesus. As He and God were one.

The time is coming, soon, when the Holy Spirit will be removed from earth. At the same time, active Christians will be Rapture and our contact will not be broken with the Holy Spirit.

But for the left behind they will feel this abandonment and be totally surprised by this feeling. These are the ones who will make the effort to correct their attitudes towards works during the Great Tribulation to become Wheat.

These righteous Wheat will be in the 1st Harvest also called the 1st Resurrection. The Wheat did not accept the Mark of the Beast and were killed.

Remember the two Harvests are of the dead individuals

1. First is for righteous
2. Second is for unrighteous.

✝

❧ CHAPTER 10 ❧

Wicked Husbandmen

Pre-Parable Information

These parables coverers a great deal of time. It reveals a period from creation to ending. It involves several classifications of types of individuals throughout history. So, look for the *clues* that will indicate to you the meanings of this parable. . will see the three (3) times the householder tries to claim his agreed portion from the husbandmen.

Matthew 21:33 *"Hear another parable: There was a certain householder, which planted a vineyard, and hedged it round about, and digged a winepress in it, and built a tower, and let it out to husbandmen, and went into a far country:"*

Here we see the householder (owner) who created a perfect place to plant grapes (earth). Everything a farmer would need to grow a good crop. He must have the desire to produce a good harvest, so he gave the renters an excellent foundation to provide an excellent financial gain for both He and the farmers. And then the owner left.

This householder is God, who has created the earth's Garden of Eden. It was beautiful and had mature plants for Adam to eat. The tell moves forward in time to Adam's failure, to when God left Adam's presence. During this period, good men tried to do good, and Enoch and Noah were two, But the farmers ignored Noah to their peril. And Noah was the last of the good men. And the Garden of Eden was also removed, but not earth. And renters had to start over again on the garden of this planet.

The next verse moves forward to a sizable number of years. The Law was given to Moses, and he gave it to the Hebrews. God gives the farmers the rules for growing grapes. These rules were when the Hebrews devised the worship plan to grow grapes (Salvation plan by works). Works continued for about 1,500 years. Many who tried to express new information were shunned, while these grapes (people) were becoming more knowledgeable in the Torah. The grapes are nearly ripe for harvesting (the end of time). Works were still the main thrust for the Hebrew religion. Many people performed works but without a heart of love. So now, we have reached the time for God to reveal the truth for salvation. A new covenant is about to come to the farmers.

Matthew 21:34, *"And when the time of the fruit drew near, he sent his servants to the husbandmen, that they might receive the fruits of it."*

Many individuals are not aware of these servants. After Adam came some good people who worship God, but over time they became less and less until there was only Noah and his family. We are not given the words spoken by Noah, but he preached for 120 years about their evil ways, and they ignored His prediction of the flood. After the flood came John the Baptist who was preaching different, more correct doctrine about Jesus. John and many more prophets were killed by the influence of the Priest, Rabbis, Pharisees, and royalties. But this fruit too was going to get ripe.

Matthew 21:35 *"And the husbandmen took his servants, and beat one, and killed another, and stoned another."*

Here we read of these husbandmen who have treated these servants of God. These are supposedly righteous men who punished God's servants.

There is the time the Temple Priest had gotten so power-hungry they would do anything to keep their prestige and power over the grapes (Hebrews). *"Power corrupts, and absolute power corrupts absolutely."* But the husbandman continues to try to get his due (souls).

Matthew 21:36 *"Again, he sent other servants more than the first: and they did unto them likewise."*

This second time is like the first time; treated just the same. These acts become a little more obvious who these servants of God are. They are the apostles. Even though the Apostles came with Jesus, God wants to present them here along with the other sacrifices. And another group of Missionaries will follow these later in life.

Matthew 21:37 *"But last of all he sent unto them his son, saying. They will reverence my son."*

This statement might make us wonder about this householder logic. But God is all-knowing, and His ways are not our ways. If He does not send his son, there will be no salvation by faith. This salvation by faith goes back to Abraham's sacrifice of his son Isaac. The Hebrew people knew this but did not associate it with salvation.

Matthew 21:38 *"But when the husbandmen saw the son, they said among themselves, This is the heir; come, let us kill him, and let us seize on his inheritance."*

Now we get to the heart of this parable. These husbandmen show their evil actions, as do the lost in our generation. They appear to think if they keep doing the thing that does not work, it will eventually work. They deceive themselves. They obviously do not know the Law that says only the family of the householder can inherit. And we who belong to Jesus can inherit along with Jesus, all that God possess, everything!

Matthew 21:39 *"And they caught him, and cast* him out of the vineyard, and slew him.*"*

We know this is Jesus being captured in the Garden of Gethsemane before his illegal trial. To be cast out of the vineyard is paramount to be thrown out of this world, the vineyard. Jesus was cast out of Jerusalem to be murdered on Golgotha. This event was God's logic in his plan for man. We all can consider ourselves husbandman, as it is because of our sins that Jesus had to die. The following is a question for you and me. What would be your judgment now for this betrayal?

Matthew 21:40 *"When the lord therefore of the vineyard cometh, what will he do unto those husbandmen?"*

What is the vineyard? It is the earth. The vine is God's created salvation systems (do good, obey Law, faith only, and deeds). The fruit is those saved souls of God's vineyard. So, who are the husbandmen? They primarily are the Church's infested false leaders. However, it is everyday people who use the Christians for profit, power, status, and personal gain, but not for Christ's Kingdom.

Matthew 21:41 *"They say unto him, He will miserably <u>destroy those wicked men</u>, and <u>will let out</u> his vineyard unto other husbandmen, which shall render him the fruits in their seasons."*

The *"let out his vineyard unto another"* is to Jesus and His 1,000-year Kingdom. *The husbandmen are the bride, the Church, to help save. souls during Jesus' Kingdom.*

They, the Raptured alive Church, will be instrumental in saving the children and those who grow into adulthood, from their adult parent survivors of War #1. Sin will still be present in Jesus' Kingdom but not form Satan as he is locked up in the Abyss. And the ones who sin will not be allowed in Jerusalem, Jesus' capital city.

✝

CHAPTER 11

The Good Samaritan

L uke 10 25—37 "*(25) And, behold, a certain lawyer stood up, and tempted him, saying, Master, what shall I do to inherit eternal life? (26) He said unto him, What is written in the law? how readest thou? (27) And he answering said, Thou shalt love the Lord thy God with all thy heart, and with all thy soul, and with all thy strength, and with all thy mind; and thy neighbour as thyself. (28) And he said unto him, Thou hast answered right: this do, and thou shalt live. (29) But he, willing to justify himself, said unto Jesus, And who is my neighbour? (30) And Jesus answering said, A* certain man* went down from Jerusalem to Jericho, and fell among thieves, which stripped him of his raiment, and wounded *him, and* departed, leaving him half dead. *(31) And by chance there came down a certain priest that way: and when he saw him, he passed by on the other side. (32) And likewise a Levite, when he was at the place, came and looked on him, and passed by on the other side. (33) But a certain Samaritan, as he journeyed, came where he was: and when he saw him, he had compassion on him, (34) And went to him, and bound up his wounds, pouring in oil and wine, and set him on his own beast, and brought him to an inn, and took care of him. (35) And on the morrow when he departed, he took out two pence, and gave them to the host, and said unto him, Take care of him; and whatsoever thou spendest more, when I come again, I will repay thee. (36) Which now of these three, thinkest thou, was neighbour unto* *him that fell among the thieves? (37) And he said, He that shewed mercy on him. Then said Jesus unto him, Go, and do thou likewise."*

Notice this lawyer is trying to catch Jesus in some sort of trick. He is hoping Jesus will error in some way of God's Laws, for the Law required certain positive acts and certain negative acts. *The Traditions of the Elders were so powerful they were as strong as the Law.* One tradition was that no one was to have anything to do with the Samaritans, who were half Jew and half gentile.

In those days, there was a tradition where Jews could only marry inside the Jewish family. The Jews hated Samaritans for disobeying that tradition. So, Jesus is casting a righteous trap for this lawyer. So, Jesus lays the bait for the lawyer.

"What is written the law? And the esteemed lawyer quickly replies with *"Love the Lord thy God"* and *"thy neighbor as thyself."* Then the lawyer trying to justify himself by asking, *"And who is my neighbour?"* He now has just opened the door for Jesus to answer his trick question.

Jesus' answer is direct and to the point for an active mind knowing God's law. Jesus is about to take advantage of the traditions against Samarians. In *Jesus' story, he uses two religious leaders, the priest, and a Levite.* The priest worked in God's temple, and the Levites trained to become a priest, as the only priest could come from the Levite tribe.

If anyone should be helpful to a person in need, it should be these men of God. Keep in mind at this time in history; these men still have the Knowledge of Good and Evil, but not the Holy Spirit.

Here we are given a story by Jesus for us to learn from too. A non-Samaritan () was on a journey from Jerusalem to Jericho and was in an open country where he was robbed and beaten by thieves, and they left him to die

A Priest came by and avoided the man. Next came a Levite who looked but did not help the dying man. Here we see the effects of the uncompassionate Priest and Levite of avoiding this injured man. To the Priest and Levite, this man was unworthy of being helped. What happened to *"Love thy neighbor as thy self"*?

Jesus is now striking a point of contention against traditions (not a law). Now we are passing from carnality to spirituality knowledge. If the priest and the Levite had God's Laws written on their hearts, they would have stopped and helped this dying man? In Exo.22, We read Moses Law about how a *stranger was not to be vexed*.

Exodus 22:21 *"Thou shalt neither vex a stranger, nor oppress him: for ye were strangers in the land of Egypt."*

The word *vex* means = *"yaw-naw,'* a prim. root; *to rage or violent;* by impl. to *suppress* to *maltreat:* -destroy, (thrust out by) oppress (-ing, -ion. or), proud, vex, do violence.[1]"

Surely this lawyer knew this law, too, plus the law written in Exo. 23.

Exodus 23:9 *"Also thou shalt not oppress a stranger: for ye know the heart of a stranger, seeing ye were strangers in the land of Egypt."*

Several scripture laws refer to the care of animals of strangers and an enemy. And it would indicate that care of animals would also infer God's children too.

But remember, the Holy Spirit has not come to earth yet, but those two men did know good and evil. And they chose evil. Why? *"How think ye?"*

Most traditions are *non-Biblical,* but they can carry the power of the law if repeated often enough. Here we see the priest and Levite avoiding the dying man. Is it because he is a Samaritan, or is it due to their fear, if seen, of any reprisals of the Chief Priest, due to the inbreed disrespect of the Samaritans?

The latter seems the most correct. We today experience this same effect with our traditions and lack of respect for other human beings. How do you feel when approached by a beggar or a homeless person? How about a Hell's Angels biker or any gang?

Prejudice is a haunting condition that stems from past teachings, experiences, or fears. Our experiences have taught us to be careful around specific individuals. If it looks like a duck, quacks like a duck, swims like a duck ----- it is a duck! However, it could be a Swan!

As our world gets increasingly evil, the more skeptical and suspicious we get. These feelings are God-given to help us avoid evil and dangerous situations. However, God also gave us compassion to exercise too. Herewith the Samaritan, it is obvious the injured man is in danger of losing his life. *Now place yourself in this situation!*

The injured man is helpless, and no others are around to help. So, fear of reprisal should not stop you from helping the man. Today the Good Samaritan Law should protect you legally. Today we can call for assistance on cell phones, but if no contact is available, we can carefully place the injured in our car and drive to help. But, if you see someone broken down on the highway, *be careful*; call for help before you get out of your locked car. This situation could be dangerous, especially if it is a young or middle-aged woman. Her male companion could hide in the back seat. If you see a male rise up, drive off but seek help for them from the Highway Patrol.

Matthew 10:16 *"Behold, I send you forth as sheep in the midst of wolves: be ye therefore <u>wise as serpents</u>, and <u>harmless as doves.</u>"*

Now let us return to the Two Religious Men.

Both of these religious men, the priest, and Levite, appear to be taught prejudice from old traditions to avoid those *"worthless Samaritans."* This legacy of hatred has been passed down by Satan ever since Adam's time, where Cain slew Abel (Gen. 4). Cain had only one law to obey, *"do good,"* not evil. The same conditions exist for us today.

We a given the Holy Spirit to guide us, but we must be sensitive to his leading. The world has given us a name for this, and it is called *our conscience.* Satan makes fun of this gift by placing the red devil on one shoulder and a white angel on the other shoulder. And they are giving conflicting information to their host. This dilemma requires the host to know the difference between what is right and what is evil.

Therefore, without Biblical knowledge (lust of the flesh and lust of the eyes) to solve this dilemma, Satan will lead us towards evil, *for we are evil-bent people.*

This parable reveals how critical is the condition of one's heart. It is not that important as to how we are treated, but how we treat others. *We are not responsible for the sins of others, only for our sins!* Unless we are the perpetrator of that sin.

When a person needs help, it is the Christian's responsibility to give that help, regardless of race, social position, male or female, rich or poor, Christian or not. This Good Samaritan had compassion for this man and did what he could to help him, even though this man may have hated the Samaritans.

Today there is such a need for Christians to act to help those in need. Our society is not with the needy, be it self-induced or not. The government has taken on the responsibility of providing free help, *which is being abused by the un-needy.* In their selfishness or laziness, they continue to think they deserve government pay-outs.

The government is unable to monitor those who are and who are not in need. When the Church supported this need, there was accountability by those in need of the Church. The abuse, if present, would be short-lived. Being responsible to friends and neighbors has more force than to an impersonal government.

At present, people are not concerned about their reputation as in the past. A man's word was his bond, but this bond's abuse has caused much skepticism in relationships. To borrow money today, you must have some kind of equity greater than the amount to borrow. Even then, the loaner must inspect the loan's use, as it must be adequate results to retain the value borrowed. If the borrower defaults, the loaner must be able to recover his loan value by the equity.

CHAPTER 12

The Sheep from the Goats and Wheat from the Tares

Keep in mind that Matthew 24 and 25 were answers to Jesus' questions from the Apostles (in Mat. 24:3) about the end of the world.

Matthew.25:31–46 "(31) *When the <u>Son of man shall come</u> in his glory, and all the holy angels with him, then shall he sit upon the throne of his glory: (32) And before him shall be gathered all nations: <u>and he shall separate them one from another,</u> as a <u>shepherd divideth his sheep from the goats</u>: (33) And he shall set the sheep on his right hand, but the goats on the left. (34) Then shall the King say unto them on his right hand, Come, ye blessed of my Father, inherit the kingdom prepared for you from the foundation of the world:_(35) For I was an hungered, and ye gave me meat: I was thirsty, and ye gave me drink: I was a stranger, and ye took me in: (36) Naked and ye clothed me: I was sick, and ye visited me: I was in prison, and ye came unto me. (37) Then shall the righteous answer him, saying, Lord, when saw we thee an hungered, and fed* **thee***? or thirsty, and gave* **thee** *drink? (38) When saw we thee a stranger, and took* thee in? or naked, and clothed **thee***? (39) Or when saw we thee sick, or in prison, and came unto thee? <u>(40) And the King shall answer and say unto them, Verily I say unto you, Inasmuch as ye have done</u>* it <u>unto one of the least of these my brethren, ye have done it unto me. (41) Then shall he say also unto them on the left hand, Depart from me,</u>*

ye cursed, into everlasting fire, prepared for the devil and his angels:
(42) For I was an hungered, and ye gave me no meat: I was thirsty,
and ye gave me no drink: (43) I was a stranger, and ye took me not
in: naked, and ye clothed me not: sick, and in prison, and ye visited
me not. (44) Then shall they also answer him, saying, Lord, when
saw we thee an hungered, or athirst, or a stranger, or naked, or sick,
or in prison, and did not minister unto thee? (45) Then shall he
answer them, saying, Verily I say unto you, Inasmuch as ye did it *not*
to one of the least of these, ye did it *not to me. (46) And these shall go*
away into punishment: but the righteous into life eternal."

In Matthew 25: 31–46 lies the story or parable of the sheep and goats.
It appears in Mat.25:25 as it is an essential concept for us to grasp. It
goes hand in hand with the previous verses of scriptures. But it will
take a few scriptures to get the *clues,* but please read all these verses for
complete understanding. We must pause and see the differences leading
to the sheep and goats.

If we go back to the Old Testament, we will read that both the sheep
and goats are righteous sacrifices to be used in the Day of Atonement to
atone for that year's sins. If a person had only goats, he could sacrifice
the goat. So why this separation? (Lev. 3:12)

First, we must understand the characteristics of both animals. These
characteristics are essential to this dissertation. See if you can recognize
some of these animal traits in a group of humans.

Goat's Behaviors

Goats are the more difficult of the two to control. They are used for milk, meat, furs, and skins. Their behavior includes:

1. They are curious creatures.
2. They like to explore.
3. They are mountain climbers, especially the Rams.
4. They are more independent.
5. They are excellent escape artists.
6. They are hard to contain.
7. They spread out rather than stay close together.
8. The Rams have variable length horns.
9. They will attack predators.
10. They will establish a hierarchy.
11. They try to eat everything. They can eat some poisonous plants without effects.

Sheep Behavior

Sheep are more easily controlled of the two. And they are used in much the same way as goats, but their fur is exceptionally useful. Their behavior is different than the goats. Here are some:

1. They are not curious animals.
2. They only move for more food, grasses, and water.
3. They are not particularly good climbers.
4. They are very dependent animals.
5. They are not good at escaping due to their together needs.
6. They are easy to contain.
7. They generally stay close.
8. They have small horns.
9. They will run from predators unless trapped.

10. They will establish a hierarchy, but 1st sheep who moves they will follow.
11. They are more particular about their food.

The sheep are the preferred creature to have due to their ease in controlling. You can say sheep are more obedient. They also are not the brightest animal of the two. However, their fur is a valuable asset. These sheep are more obedient creatures. So, it can be said the sheep are not aggressive, more compliant, know their place, try to stay together, and follow their Sheppard. The goats are more aggressive, wander off looking for new things, difficult to pin up, self-serving, and follow the lead goat.

In Joh.10, we read the unmistakable position of the sheep. And other scriptures reveal this also.

John 10:14–15 *"(14) I am the good shepherd, and know my sheep, and am known of mine. (15) as the Father knoweth me, even so know I the Father: and I lay down my life for the sheep."*

This verse is self-explanatory. Jesus knows his sheep, which are those who believe in Jesus' salvation. Jesus is the Son of God, died to pay for our sins, rose from the dead, is at the right hand of God, and will come back for us to take us to Heaven. Christians are these sheep.

There are other sheep who will be converted to Jesus during the Great Tribulation and are called the Tribulation Saints. Being persuaded by proof and not blind Faith, they are called "Wheat." Both Church and Tribulation Saints must always reflect Jesus' light, even in dangerous times, Mat.5.

Mathew 5:16 *"Let your light so shine before men, that they may see your good works, and glorify your Father which is in heaven."*

It is clear from this verse of scripture that your light is affected by *good works. If there are no good works, there is no good, reflected light.* Therefore, this applies to the five virgins (unrighteous) who are without light or good works (Mat.25). Are these five unprepared righteous virgins who are saved by faith alone? Yes, but without works, what will happen to them? These words are written to the five unprepared virgins.

Matthew 25:13 "*Watch, therefore, for ye know neither the day nor the hour wherein the Son of man cometh.*"

These words repeated in many different scriptures are about the thief's coming in the night. This statement is about Jesus' *2nd Return in the air* to Rapture the Church. His 3rd Return will be with bells and whistles and not like a thief. This Rapture is the 2nd Return in the air, and the unprepared virgins (goats) *are left behind due to a lack of good works (no light).* We will further read of a lord on a trip to a foreign land in Mat.25.

Matthew 25:13–29 follows with the Parable of the Talents, where a lord (Jesus) is traveling (after his crucifixion) into a far country (Heaven). He gives each of his servants (Apostles, Christians, and ½ christians) three different amounts of talents. The first two (Apostles and Christians) invested their talents (works) and produced a higher profit (souls) for their lord. The third servant (½ christians) just buried (no works) his talent yielding nothing, not even interest for his lord. When that lord (Jesus) returns, there is an accounting (Judgment Seat of Christ) for deeds and results. The Lord rewards those individuals for their performance *except the lazy servant who is without works.* Notice what the Lord (Jesus) does to the unprofitable servant in verse 30.

Matthew 25:30 "*And cast ye the unprofitable servant into outer darkness: there shall be weeping and gnashing of teeth.*"

This *"weeping and gnashing of teeth"* is not the Lake of Fire but a place of undesirable conditions. *Weeping* is the realization of missing something they were told about but ignored. The *"gnashing of teeth"* is the pain and utter discomfort and deeds they must now do for salvation.

The *"gnashing of teeth"* is their feeling of embarrassment and not being permitted into Jesus' city Zion (Jerusalem) during those 1,000 years. This anger will fester in darkness and will create opposition to Jesus' rulership, which Satan will use to gather an army against Jesus after His 1,000-year Kingdom. This is the time Satan is paroled out of the Abyss.

In the Great Tribulation, death is behind every door and is constantly stalking and catching some Wheat. This event is a metaphor for their experiences during those seven years during the Great Tribulation. The outer darkness is revealing the evil that will come from outside the Church (Satan). This darkness refers to the evil Satan, who is the evil power, which causes God to bring wrath on earth for seven years. Christians call it the Great Tribulation.

Here again, *some are saved by Faith but without good deeds.* This subject is so important to Jesus that he continues his dialog with the separation of the sheep from the goats starting in verse 31.

Now back to Matthew 25:31–51

In <u>verse 31</u>, we read of Jesus' 3rd Return to earth and sits on his throne of Glory. With him are the Bride and all the angels, not some but all obedient angels. This return will not be like a thief in the night.

In <u>verse 32</u>, it reveals the gathering of all nations, which is Jesus' 3rd Return. This occurrence is supported by his ordering the collection of all nations. It is here Jesus reveals two distinct groups. One is the sheep, the other the goats.

In <u>Verse 33–34</u>, Jesus will set the sheep on his right (the honored hand), and they will "*inherit the Kingdom from the foundation of the world.*" In the old world, you never ate or touched anyone with your left hand. And this custom continues today in certain areas.

This time is when Christians (right) will inherit all God possesses, and they will come into the Jesus' Kingdom prepared from the beginning of the earth. This inheritance reveals God's reward is for man before the creation of the universe.

In <u>verses 35–40,</u> God reveals the deeds man has performed for other needy individuals will be remembered. The goats (separated at the Rapture) are the Tribulation Saints save by faith after the Rapture but left behind. They now realize they must do the deeds to be fed with meat (knowledge), drink pure water of righteousness, housing (make weak bodies strong), clothing by washing away sins (Baptism) for the righteous act of the Saints. Also, care for the sick (lost) and visit those trapped in Satan's and man's prison.

In doing so, the Tribulation Goats, by proven Faith and now through Deeds, have become sheep (also called Wheat). During the Great Tribulation, the goat's transformation from goats to Sheep is revealed in the parable of the Wheat and Tares. But what of the unconverted Hebrews to Faith in Jesus and those <u>Tribulation Saints without deeds</u>? Verse 37.

Matthew 25:37 "*Then shall he say also unto them <u>on the left hand,</u> <u>Depart from me, ye cursed, into everlasting fire,</u> prepared for the devil and his angels:*"

This departure speaks of the Great White Throne Judgment of God. But there is a slight *twist during Jesus' 1,000-year Kingdom.* The left-behind Tribulation Saints and the 144,000 Hebrew missionaries of Rev. 7 will convert the Hebrew nation to Jesus.

As these converts and deedful Tribulation Saints are now called Wheat and those who reject (Blaspheme the Holy Spirit), Jesus is the Tares to be pulled up and cast into the fire (Lake of Fire). This

Wheat and Tares parable is to occur during Jesus' 1,000-year Kingdom. During the 1,000 years, new children will be born to Tribulation Saint's survivors of Armageddon. And children will be born to those children, too. The sin nature will continue during Jesus' Kingdom through these mortal children. It is here the Wheat (righteous), and the Tares (unrighteous) will be separated. You will see this at the end of the parable of the Wheat from the Tares, Mat.13: 37–40.

Matthew. 13:37–40 "*(37)* *He answered and said unto them, He that soweth the good seed is the Son of man; (38) The field is the world; the good seed are the children of the kingdom, but the tares are the children of the wicked* **one***; (39) The enemy that sowed them is the devil; the harvest is the end of the world;* [2nd Harvest] *and the reapers are the angels. (40) Therefore the tares are gathered* [2nd Harvest] *and burned in the fire; so shall it be in the end of this world.*"

Note
You can find these two harvests in Rev.14:12–20.

The *1st clue* is, "*soweth the good seed is the Son of Man.*" Jesus came to earth to sow the good seeds of a new covenant for man's salvation. Therefore, these verses refer to Jesus' life and his effects on individuals to the end of the earth. And will include the: Church Saints, the Tribulation Saints, and the righteous children born during the 1,000 years.

The *2nd clue* is "*the children of the Kingdom.*" There are two thoughts here: 1) is the world includes all children chosen (past and present) from the duration of the world; 2) the kingdom is the 1,000-year Kingdom of Jesus. But verse 39 disputes number 1 by indicating "*the harvest is the end of this world*" This harvest is the 2nd Harvest of Rev.14:17–20.

Some scholars see this harvest as occurring at Armageddon. However, if one looks at the words *"the children of the kingdom"* purely, then this harvest of souls is during Jesus' earthly kingdom, which is Jesus' 1,000-year Kingdom. This harvest is also supported by *"the end of the world,"* which comes after Jesus' 1,000-year Kingdom and Rev.20:15. And God's War #2 with the paroled Satan and his fallen away army.

LESSONS LEARNED

As you can see in these verses of scripture, works are required. The whole Mat. 25 revealing deeds from:

1. The virgins (faithful) to keep revealing their righteous acts, both verbal and physical) before the unrighteous.
2. If no works or deeds, expect to be left behind.
3. The servants receiving talents are expected to produce for God.
4. If no increase of souls in Jesus' kingdom by given talents, expect to be cast into the Great Tribulation. You are saved by faith but have no treasures.
5. For those of them who will not help our fellow man (with carnal and spiritual help) during the Great Tribulation, they have fallen away. Their heart is without love for their brothers. Fear has affected their faith in Jesus, and they will accept the Mark of the Beast, thereby becoming the Tares, and will be cast into the Lake of Fire (Mat.25: 41–46).

One last <u>*clue*</u> for you to consider is the first two righteous servants <u>spoken to by the *"lord."*</u> But the last servant (unrighteous) <u>was spoken to by the *"King."*</u>

The word for lord here is = *"koo'-ree-os; from* kurŏs (*supremacy*); *supreme* in authority, i.e. (as a noun) *controller*; by impl, *Mr.* (as a respectful title): -God, Lord, master, sir[1]."

This King is God speaking to his righteous children. These individuals were saved by Faith and Deeds. A more severe *clue* is here for you to see in Mat. 25:30–31 verses Mat. 25:45–46.

Matthew 25:30—31 *"(30) <u>And cast ye the unprofitable servant into outer darkness: there shall be weeping and gnashing of teeth.</u> (31) When the Son of man shall come in his glory, and all the holy angels with him, then shall he sit upon the throne of his glory:"*

Matthew 25:45–46 *"(45) Then shall he answer them, saying, Verily I say unto you, Inasmuch as ye did* it *not to one of the least of these, ye did* it *not to me. (46) <u>And these shall go away into everlasting punishment: but the righteous into life eternal.</u>"*

Here we see two distinct types of punishments for the same kind of individuals. They both have not done the deeds of Jesus (God). Notice the first punish is before Jesus comes to sit on his throne. This point is to Jesus' 2nd Return to Rapture, his righteous children.

The "*Son of man <u>shall come</u> in his glory...-to sit upon his throne*" on earth is pointing to Jesus' 3rd Return for the Jesus 1,000-years Kingdom. This event is when the unprofitable survivors (saved by faith) of the Great Tribulation have children who reject Jesus.

These will not be permitted inside Jerusalem's city or Jesus' throne during the 1,000 years. They will weep and gnash their teeth in their punishment. This chastisement of God is for the left behind, who still refused to do deeds before the Great Tribulation. But they can always do charitable deeds during the Kingdom.

But the sinful nature of these children will be present during the 1,000 years Kingdom. Therefore, those left behind can, and some will do honorable deeds in Jesus' Kingdom. During the 1,000 years, these workers will become the Wheat, versus the Tares of Mat.13:24–31.

<u>Mat. 25:45–46</u> make it clear that those *who did no deeds* for God's children are those who have not performed for God and His children But, how can they maintain faith during the Great Tribulation? These words are somewhat of a mystery. These are the *deedless christians who may not have been spiritually challenged into accepting or rejecting the Mark of the Beast.* Without this challenge, they are saved by their Faith. They were left behind by Satan too.

THE CONVERTS TO SATAN

Satan will have converts to evil after his release from the Abyss, after his 1,000 years of incarceration. Remember, the sinful nature will be present in the children of the Great Tribulation's mortal survivors. These children who reject Jesus will eventually become the army of Satan (Rev.20 7–15).

This army of Satan will bring in the ultimate end to evil on this earth. In Rev. 20:10, we read of God's loss of patience because God himself brings destruction to all evil of Satan and his army. And they are sent to the Lake of Fire (Rev. 20:15). This statement also agrees with Mat. 25:46.

Eternity begins: all evil is destroyed; God's huge city comes to earth; all nations can walk in the city. We shall see his face and not die; there will be the river of life, the Tree of Life with fruit, no night, no evil will ever be present, no sickness, no sorrows, no pain, joy abounding, and unbelievable LOVE. A WIN, WIN!!!!!!!

MATTHEW 24:30–51 VERSES MATTHEW 25: 41–46

It is necessary to see the relationship between these verses of scripture. Both chapters (24/25) are about the same event but show different concepts.

Verse 30 reveals Jesus is coming in his glory. This coming is not the silent Rapture like a thief in the night. But in his glory, the 3rd Return to establish His 1,000-year Kingdom. It will come with all the bells and whistles. For the lost, this will be invaders from space. However, they (the lost) will recognize Jesus is coming to destroy them.

In Verse 31, first, Jesus gathers his elect, both Jew and gentile. Notice these are collected from both *earth* and *Heaven*. Earth is the Tribulation Saints, and Heaven is all previous Saints (Old Testament and Church). This gathering is to show us that Jesus has kept His promises.

Verse 32 is moving to the future with a *clue* for us to recognize when this gathering will take place. Jesus uses a parable to reveal the time this event will occur. And He uses the Fig Tree Parable. The fig tree produces fig every year, so what year could we nail down to know Jesus' return? Verse 33 refers to the information found in Chapters Mat. 24 and 25. So when you see these events occurring, know that the time for the Rapture is near.

In verse 34, Jesus reveals the time generation for these events. He uses the word generation. This word used in Jesus' day could mean forty or seventy years. Forty was the space for birthing children, and seventy was the time for life. Seventy years reveals best the time of average death. Today insurance actuaries place our life span in the seventies, and Jesus tells us we will have life for 70 years or 80 if we are strong (Psl. 90:10).

Note

Therefore, we are within this time frame of the Rapture. If we return to verses 32 and 33, we can see how they agree with how close we are to the Rapture.

Verses 37–39 support this period by revealing the sinful conditions in Noah's day to the sinful condition at the Rapture day. Their sins were a normal inbred condition practiced every minute of every day. So much so, God destroyed them. If you stop and study the sinful conditions of today, you will know the time is near.

Verses 40–42 Show an after-the-fact *clue*. There, two different people in two different situations where one is taken and one left behind. These two verses show the removal of Christians in their typical workday. The left behind is the Pew-Sitters or non-working ½ christians. *This event is to motivate the left behind ½ christians to go through the Great Tribulation for their last chance for salvation.*

You have read of the characteristics of the sheep versus goats. Sheep follow the leader, where goats follow themselves. The goats are the *Tribulation Saints save by faith.* But they now realize they must do the deeds to feed with meat (knowledge), drink pure water of righteousness, housing (make weak bodies strong), clothing by washing away sins (Baptism) for the righteous act of the Saints, care for the sick (lost) and visit those trapped in Satan's and man's prisons. In doing so, the Tribulation Goats by Faith and now Deeds have become ~~sheep~~ (Wheat). The word sheep is reserved for Church Saints. These unconverted goats *are the Tribulation pew-sitters* that were faced with the decision to accept or reject the Mark of the Beast, and they took the Mark of the Beast and have submitted to Satan, they are called Tares.

Verses 43–45, here again, we look after the fact. Jesus uses the word IF. If you do the study of God's Word, Christians would have known approximately the time of Jesus' 2nd Return. This is like when a doctor tells his patient, *"if only you had come to me a month ago."* Therefore, Jesus is telling us the month before.

Verses 46–47 is attempting to encourage the righteous person to continue in his work for Jesus' Kingdom. Also, notice these words are for both servants, servants of Jesus.

<u>Verses 48–50</u> speaks of the evil servant. This servant has not read or studied the Beatitudes in his Bible. Here we are shown the Half-righteous servant. He is saved by faith but refuses to do the works commanded by Jesus. This servant does not know the Rapture or believes it will not come (2 Pet.3:4).

<u>Verse 51</u> ends the chapter by revealing the chastisement of this wayward servant. Notice he is placed with the hypocrites (non-believers) claiming to be believers. These are the left behind for the Great Tribulation due to the *"weeping and gnashing of teeth."* These words reveal the Great Tribulation and not the Lake of Fire.

I hope you caught the different rewards shown in Mat.24:51 versus Mat.25:46. Verse 51 speaks to not being permitted into Jesus' city or in Torment. Verse 46 shows the unrighteousness to the Lake of Fire, but the righteous into life eternal. These two points are two separate times.

LESSONS LEARNED

1. **T**he Rapture is the separation of the righteous sheep (Church Saints) from the deedless goats (Tribulation Saints).
2. The goats repent and do deeds and become righteous (Wheat)
3. The Jews convert to Jesus, and they too become Wheat.
4. The continuous 1st Harvest (dead) is during the 1,000-year Kingdom separation of the Tribulation Saints (goats) and Jews (Wheat) from the Tares. Evil's destination is Torment, and Righteous destination to Jesus' Kingdom.
5. The continuous 2nd Harvest (dead) is lost souls (Tares) during Jesus' 1,000-year Kingdom. Destine to the Lake of Fire.

✝ CHAPTER 13 ✥

Hidden Treasure

Pre-scripture Information

I want you first to understand the value of hidden treasures. God has taken the time to show you how valuable these hidden treasures will be for your enjoyment in eternity. And in doing so, we will go to the parable of Mat.13.

Mat.13:44-46 (44) Again, the <u>kingdom of heaven</u> is like unto treasure hid in a field; the which when a man hath found, he hideth, and for joy thereof goeth and selleth all that he hath, and buyeth that field. (45) Again, the kingdom of heaven is like unto a merchant man, seeking goodly pearls: (46) Who, when he had found one pearl of great price, went and sold all that he had, and bought it.

In <u>verse 44,</u> notice that it speaks of the kingdom in Heaven. This reveals how important these treasures will be to you getting to, or during eternity. This is God way of trying to impress us with just how important and enjoyable these unknown treasures will be to us. He is using something we may have experienced in our lifetime to show what is important to humans on earth.

Many individuals went to the gold fields in the 1800"s to find gold. Some were remarkably successful. Many have gone to Las Vegas to seek their fortune, and we have searcher in the sea and on the surface seeking treasures. So, God uses the attitude to reveal heavenly treasures.

The first is the searchers of the earth surface and finds an extremely valuable treasure. But he does not have available money to extract it from the ground. What would you do in this case? What he did. He hides the find until he can file a claim and sell all he owns to buy the land. If this is inadequate for understanding, God gives us another example.

<u>Verse 45</u> continues by telling of jeweler looking for jewels and finding a pear of the greatest value ever found. As a merchant he has money to invest but this pearl exceeds his resources. He does the same as the first individual. The value is greater than what he has with him, so he goes and sells all he owns.

What would your family think of you selling your home, clothing, your business, both cars, cell phones, and computers; all they enjoy for an oyster. Whatever you produce, it better be good, but do not cash in your life insurance.

You will notice God continue value dissertation with the Net parable we have looked at before. This attempt by God, will slid past many Christians. They will remain comfortable in their pew. It will go unnoticed until they see what they have missed, especially the Rapture. Then come the Great Tribulation where they will have to do deeds. The worst will be deciding to reject the Mark of Satan and be killed by Jesus; or reject the Mark of Satan and be killed by Satan. The first is for eternity the second is not eternal but mortal.

If you are faced with this decision in the near future; take the mortal death and come with us Christians into Heaven and into immortality with all your treasures. You are going to die anyway so, chose wisely!

It is absolutely imperative you understand Salvation comes by FAITH but Treasures com by Deeds (works).

Also remember Jesus' coming is like a thief in the night. Which few individuals will be looking for the clues to his coming. If they were, there would be no need for this warning.

⨎ CHAPTER 14 ⨏

The Rich Fool

Luke 12:16–21

Luke 12:16 And he spake a parable unto them, saying, The ground of a certain rich man brought forth plentifully: (17) And he thought within himself, saying, What shall I do, because I have no room where to bestow my fruits? (18) And he said, This will I do: I will pull down my barns, and build greater; and there will I bestow all my fruits and my goods.(19) And I will say to my soul, Soul, thou hast much goods laid up for many years; take thine ease, eat, drink, and be merry. (20) But God said unto him, Thou fool, this night thy soul shall be required of thee: then whose shall those things be, which thou hast provided? (21) So is he that layeth up treasure for himself, and is not rich toward God.

These verses remind me of the Church of Laodicea. He is self-involved. Notice God has provided this man a large harvest. And is considering what to do with all this crop of fruit His storage areas are already full. And he plans to tear down the old storage places and build new and bigger one.

This is an exception to the crops he had normally brought into storage; He is not considering the waste of storage when the crops return to normal production again. Sometimes normal Churches forget about this parable.

This blessing came from God and something this rich man forgot or did not believe, as it was from his labor. The thought of sharing his blessing with the poor needy never entered his mind.

He could have removed last year's crop and provided that food for the Poor. While making room for the New Crop. This concept should be exercised in Churches today.

Instead, some add a bigger Church auditorium or parking areas. And not share the blessing they received with the needy. We have seen Churches grow from success and not start a new church for the new over crowing. Eventually the old money dies and the Church cannot support the maintenance of the structure. A bigger and bigger building is not what God wants.

True Great crows of Christians focused on Jesus' Gospel should bring more Christians into Jesus' Kingdom. But the fields are white for harvest in all parts of America. But too, many fields are not getting the Gospel.

Prisons are one of those white fields. A captive audience. Many not knowing what is coming next in their life. They have been taught or not taught at all about life and what come after life. They are not aware of the two dimensions in which we live. Mortal 70 to 80 years and spiritual forever.

That is a problem with the rich. Money seems to be their most important in their lives. Like the rich man in this parable, he has given no thought to his investment into his or her next life.

We the people daily take for granted the sun will rise the next morning. We will have a job for a long time. And fail to read the obituary columns of deaths of both young and old people.

Like the rich man God tells of his demise for the next day. We have only one day at a time, and it is in that day we are to store up treasures in Heaven. We have no idea what the next day will bring.

Matthew 6:24 *"No man can serve two masters: for either he will hate the one and love the other; or else he will hold to the one and despise the other. Ye cannot serve God and mammon."*

CHAPTER 15

The Fig Tree Parable

Signs of End Times

Matthew 24:32–33 *"(32) Now learn a parable of the fig tree; When his branch is yet tender, and putteth forth leaves, ye know that summer is* **nigh:** *(33) So likewise ye, when ye shall see all these things, know that it is near, even at the doors."*

Suffice it to say this parable reveals earthly <u>clues</u> that point to Jesus' Rapture of the Church Saints. It is simple in its reading but more complicated in its message.

The people in Jesus' day were knowledgeable about the Fig Tree's growth and fruit production. Here again, we see Jesus going from known information to present more in-depth spiritual information. But how could the people at Jesus' time understand the deeper meaning of this parable? Therefore, this parable is reserved until biblical knowledge will understand (**Dan. 12**).

Please open your Bible to Mat.24 to follow the verses quoted below. There are 51 verses in Mat.24, and it will be easier to move back and forth from <u>verses</u> here in the Bible.

You will read in Mat.24:3, where the apostles ask Jesus three *questions* about end times. They thought it would be one event, but it is more than one. *So, Jesus needed to explain all events leading up to God's destruction of Satan and the earth.* The answers Jesus gives will cover the time leading up to the Rapture, The Great Tribulation, and the Great White Throne Judgment. You will notice the Rapture is not mentioned first but last. Also, the sequence of events does not appear sequel. Please see the sequences of:

1. Verses 3 is the place of Jesus' 3rd Return, Mount Olive.
2. Verses 4—8 are general conditions before the Antichrist's Beast (government) is revealed.
3. Verses 9–10 speaks of the Antichrist Government.
4. Verses 11–13 reveal the False Prophet, who brings a false religion (Islam?)
5. Verse 14 tells the gospel mission of the 144,000 Jewish Missionaries to the World (Rev. 7). This event occurs during the Great Tribulation.
6. Verse 15–28 jumps ahead to the critical verses in Daniel 12:11–12, which gives the specific time and date of Jesus' 3rd Return and Armageddon.
7. Verse 29–31 jumps ahead to the Great Tribulation end and the elect's 1st Harvest.

   Then the Parable of the Fig Tree

8. Verse 34, which comes just after this Parable, says: *"this generation shall not pass* (die), *till all these things be fulfilled."* Traditionally a generation is considered 40 years, but it can also be the age of childbearing. In Old Testament times, this could be as early as in the mid-teens.
9. Verse 37–44 is covert information about the Rapture. Verse 44 information is quite different from verse 27 information. Verse 44 is the thief in the night, where verse 27 is with all the bells and whistles. Here again, you can see the sequences appear reversed.
10. Verse 45–51 these verses confirm who will be Rapture and who will be left behind to weep and gnash his or her teeth.

The time of this *Fig Tree parable* occurrence can be confusing as it covers many years. The words in <u>verses 3–8</u> is written before this Fig Tree parable in scriptures and allude to the earth's Rapture. There you will read of false rumors of Jesus' coming to the world, False Prophet, and those who fall away from Jesus before the Rapture (2nd Thes.2).

2nd Thessalonians 2:1—4 *"(1) Now we beseech you, brethren, by the coming of our Lord Jesus Christ, and by* **our gathering together unto him,** *(2) That ye be not soon shaken in mind, or be troubled, neither by spirit, nor by word, nor by letter as from us, as that the day of Christ is at hand. (3) Let no man deceive you by any means:* <u>**for that day shall not come**</u>, *except there come a* <u>**falling away first**</u>, *and* <u>**that man of sin be**</u> <u>**revealed**</u>, *the son of perdition; (4) Who opposeth and exalteth himself above all that is called God, or that is worshipped; so that he as God sitteth in the Temple of God, shewing himself that he is God."*

Note

Notice in verse 1 above that we are *"gathering together unto him"* (Jesus). This gathering is the Rapture. Next in v<u>erse 2</u> comes reassurance ("not shaken") for the Church Saints safety and signs to look for Jesus' Rapture. Next comes the <u>*clue*</u> of deception requiring Bible knowledge to defeat. <u>Verse 3,</u> following this deception, comes the <u>*clue*</u> of the *falling away* of ½ christians, and the *son of perdition*, Satan, is revealed. <u>Verse 4</u> tells of Satan's empire is established and requiring Satanic Worship and waring the Mark of the Beast.

Now Back to Matthew 24

<u>Verse 3</u> Jesus is sitting on the Mount of Olives, and his apostle comes and asks him three questions:

1. " When shall these things be?"

2. "What shall be the sign of thy coming?"
3. "And the end of the World?"

The apostles thought that Jesus' Return would be one event and not two. So, Jesus had to answer them with a long, somewhat ambiguous answer. Jesus starts from their present position and moves forward in time.

1. "When shall these things be?"

Verse 4–5 Jesus first tells them not to be deceived. For years, many well-meaning people have been trying to reveal the time of the Rapture. But they failed to realize that the Rapture will come unannounced. *It will come as a thief in the night.* However, Jesus also said there would be signs to reveal the nearness of his 2nd Return.

Furthermore, Jesus tells us many will come claiming they are the Christ, and they will deceive many. How are these *many* possible? Many are not studying their Bibles, and pastors are not revealing the nearness of time. Jesus tells us to *take heed for ourselves (study).*

Verse 6-7 Reveals many things will occur, but they are the same things that have happened to us in the past. Nothing new here! But there are famines, pestilences, earthquakes in many places. In America, some of these events are happening but slower than in other 3rd world countries.

Verse 8 These previous scriptures show Christians the clues to be looking for *Jesus' 2nd and 3rd Returns.* But here in verse 8, is addressed in 2nd Thes.2:2 *"be not shaken in mind or troubled,"* referring to Mat.24:8, *"All these are the beginning of sorrow."* Because the Church Saints will be Raptured, and the Tribulation Saint salvation will be *eternally protected.* Mathew 24 and 2nd Thes.2 go hand in hand, revealing the same events.

<u>Verse 9–10</u> When the above events grow intensely. And when this event comes, it triggers hate and betrayal in the people's attitude towards Christians. We are presently at the beginning of this event. Christians are killed in many places in the world, especially in locations dominated by Muslims.

<u>Verses 11–14</u> speaks of the period of false prophets who will deceive many, who Jesus said would come and deceive. In Verse 12, Sins will abound (grow), and Love will all but vanish. Antichrist #1 will rule in the first half of the seven years. Verse 13 is written to the Tribulation Saints to stay faithful and endure to the Great Tribulation's end for salvation awaits them. Verse 14, however, speaks of the time during the Great Tribulation where the 144,000 Jewish Missionaries convert all the Jews to Jesus, which occurs primarily in the last half of the seven years, under the rule of Antichrist #2.

<u>Verse 15</u> Has a *clue* that speaks to an event that will occur *halfway through* the Great Tribulation, supported by verse 21, which makes it apparent that the Great Tribulation is in process. But this is referring to the *last 3½ years* when Satan's statue, *"the abomination of desolation,"* is set up in God's rebuilt Temple. These last 3½ years are when Satan declares himself as god, and worship of Satan will be required (Rev. 13) for all earthlings, and this will be the most critical time of God's punishment on earth.

<u>Verses 16–20</u> tell the people, at the time the statue of Satan set up in the Temple, to leave and seek security away from Satan (Rev. 12). This escape is for those saved by Faith to leave the cities and seek isolation from Satan's requirement to accept the Mark of the Beast. But those who escape must remember the parable of the *"Lamp Under the Bowl"* on a hill!

These escapes are so vital, and time is of the essence that the Hebrews are to leave everything they possess and escape into the wilderness. This escape is supported by Rev. 12:6. Also, they, and we are to pray for no impediments to prevent them from escaping.

Verse 21–22, these words reveal the last 3½ years of the Great Tribulation. Here you will see the *wrath of Satan* and the *wrath of God* on earth. A double dose! And the dosage is so unhealthy that God must shorten the wrath for God's elect. This elect is the 144,000 and their converts. (Rev.7) This period is their second and last chance for salvation!

Verses 23–26 tell of the False Religion (1st half) that will come to power during the Great Tribulation. Here people will be mesmerized by the magic these false prophets will do. They are so good at their magic; they can almost trick the elect (Hebrews). This practice aids the False Religion, which will eventually become Satanic Worship.

Verse 27 This is Jesus' coming and not as a thief in the night. *It is with all the bells and whistles, light everywhere, and coming with Jesus will be the Old Testament Saints, the Church Saints, the Tribulation Saints, and the angels.* There will be no doubt who is coming. It will be the alien invasion revealed by the entertainment movies and TV industry for the spiritually unknowledgeable. Satan's propaganda has worked! Earthling will fight these invaders in War #1, Armageddon.

In verse 28, God reveals the dead carcass, which is the former church after the Rapture. These members are those saved by faith but have not performed deeds to grow the Church. Therefore, they are not Raptured. The left-behind church members will now know the truth of their deceiving themselves. They will be attacked by Satan's demons and challenged with *accepting or not* the Mark of the Beast. *To refuse means bodily death, and to accept the Mark means spiritual Death.* The first physical death is to Heaven, and the spiritual second Death to the Lake of Fire. *–Your decision!*

<u>Verse 29</u> Jesus now nails the time to the end of the seven years of the Great Tribulation. Darkness will be oppressive, stars falling, and the powers of the universe shaken. Notice *"immediately after"* God reveals darkness but then shall appear the *"Son of man."* This appearance is Jesus' 3rd Return with all the Saints and angles for War #1, Armageddon (Rev. 19).

2. *"What shall be the sign of thy coming?"*

Here are 2 questions in one, which can cause a dilemma as to which return, the (2nd Return) Rapture, or the 3rd Return (Armageddon)? The Rapture will be, or should be, *an excellent sign for earthlings,* but will it? Is it possible the Rapture will be very few people and explained away by Antichrist #1? From these following scriptures, it is Jesus' 3rd Return. 2nd Thes.2 is straightforward. Antichrist #1 (the son of perdition) is revealed to Christians. Perdition is Satan, Antichrist #2.

2nd Thessalonians 2:3–4 *"(3) Let no man deceive you by any means: for that day shall not come, except there come a falling away first, and that man of sin be revealed, the son of perdition; (4) Who opposeth and exalteth himself above all that is called God, or that is worshipped; so that he as God sitteth in the temple of God, shewing himself that he is God."*

<u>Verse 30</u> reveals the most ominous sign for those lost souls who heard the gospel but refused to believe, Jesus' salvation, Jesus' 3rd Return, and Armageddon. Everything makes sense to them now. They know Hell awaits them, *but not the Lake of Fire.* They see the gathering of verse 31.

<u>Verse 31</u> reveals the *gathering of all* the elect (Jews, Gentiles, Old Testament Saints, Church Saints, Tribulation Saints, and angels) *"from one end of heaven* (universe?) *to the others. "* This event occurs during the 1st Harvest of Rev.14:12–16, where all righteous Hosts are gathered into the army for Jesus. This gathering is not the Rapture! It is the

collection of righteous souls who died in the past and during the Great Tribulation.

<u>Verse 32</u> reverts back in time to reveal vital <u>*clue*</u>s for Christians and the Hebrews, a sign pointing to the time of the Rapture. Verse 36 proclaims, "*but of that day and hour knoweth no man,*" this is about the start of the Rapture to the *end of times*. These event sequences from verses 32–51 is further proof of the Rapture. Also, Jesus' 3rdReturn is revealed in Daniel for the exact day. Now we have arrived at the parable of the fig tree.

THE FIG TREE

This parable uses a Fig Tree as a metaphor to reveal the time and appearance of the Fig Tree's growth as it pertains to the time of the Rapture.

Matthew 24:32–33 "*Now learn a parable of the fig tree; When his branch is yet tender, and putteth forth leaves, ye know that summer is nigh: (33) So likewise ye, when ye shall see all these things, know that it is near,* even at the doors.*"*

Jesus is telling us to look for these events as you would for Figs. It is not complicated, just like any fruit tree has time for producing fruit. The change in the fig tree leaves will reveal when the fruit is closely following. For example, Apples are mature in August to September. These <u>*clues*</u> given before in these scriptures will also lead us to the ripe time for Jesus' 2nc Return.

For the Christian doing God's work, you need not be overly concerned with end times and be at peace. Just as when you drive the speed limit, you will have peace of no speeding ticket. However, you should be able to answer questions of people seeking answers. We are told this in 2nd Tim.2 and 3.

2ⁿᵈ Timothy

2ⁿᵈ Timothy.2:15. *"Study to shew thyself approved unto God, a workman that needeth not to be ashamed, rightly dividing the word of truth."*

2ⁿᵈ Timothy 3:1—7 *"(1) This also know that in the last days, perilous times shall come. (2) For men shall be lovers of their own selves, covetous, boasters, proud, blasphemers, disobedient to parents, unthankful, unholy, (3) Without natural affection, trucebreakers, false accusers, incontinent, fierce, despisers of those that are good, (4) Traitors, heady, highminded, lovers of pleasures more than lovers of God; (5) Having a form of godliness, but denying the power thereof: from such turn away. (6) For of this sort are they which creep into houses, and lead silly captive women laden with sins, led away with divers lusts, (7) Ever learning, and never able to come to the knowledge of the truth."*

If one's eyes are open to the Fig Tree growth, you cannot but *know our world is in the leaf budding time.* Evil is growing stronger today as never before. Governments around the world are turning away from Jesus. Christians punished for just being a Christian. The increase of ungodly pastors *"ever learning, but never able to come to the knowledge of the truth."* And *"Having a form of Godliness but denying the power."* Revealing to us the false religious leader of today who pick and choose what verses of scriptures they will follow but deny God's words' whole truth. And complete rebellion against God.

Note

Please continue studying the rest of Matthew24 as more *clues* are leading to Jesus' coming. Also, in Daniel are verses speaking the specific day of Jesus' 3rd Return.

3. *"And the end of the World?"*

Note

In Daniel 12, you can read specific days, which brings Jesus' 3rd Return to establish his 1,000-years earthly Kingdom. *The start of the end-time prophecies is* **anchored to the Rapture.** Now Jesus gives the parable of the Fig Tree to *those searchers of scriptures (five obedient virgins)* who will be given the conditions to look for to get the approximate time of Jesus' Rapture, but not the exact <u>day or hour.</u> How about the week?

I would like for you to see the importance of the mystery of the Rapture Jesus' answers to his apostles are hidden in the message that the end of time hinges around the Rapture. At that time, the people could not understand this knowledge, but we have been given insight today through the apostles and scriptures. The people then did not have all of God's words. God, in His wisdom, has given us time to collect all the scriptures, learn and share his son with the lost souls of earth. God will not punish his righteous children, and he claims this in 1stThes.5.

1st Thessalonians 5:9, *"For God hath not appointed us to wrath, but to obtain salvation by our Lord Jesus Christ."*

Isn't God, Jesus, and the Holy Spirit wonderful? They are so phenomenal we cannot graph their intellectual, power, and Love fully. How could one so perfect love all of us who are so despicable? Why are we given such great treasures for reasonable service? Why were we born in the time of Faith (the Church, the Bride of Christ)? And not in the time of

Law or the Great Tribulation? What element or purpose sanctified us for this period? Questions, questions, and more questions.

"And the end of the World." by Daniel.

Please open your Bible to Daniel 12 to follow my thoughts.

However, the definitive answer is in Daniel 12. There in <u>Verse 1</u> tells us the first *clue as to the end.*

Daniel 12:1–2 "(1) *And at that time shall Michael stand up, the great prince which standeth for the children of thy people: and <u>there shall be a time of trouble,</u> such as never was since there was a nation even to that same time: <u>and at that time thy people shall be delivered, every one that shall be found written in the book.</u> (2) And many of them that sleep in the dust of the earth shall awake, <u>some to everlasting life,</u> and <u>some to shame</u> and <u>everlasting contempt.</u>"

<u>Verse 1</u> Michael must be our general of angels for the most critical time of trouble coming to earth. He is our protector from Satan. Notice in verse 1 is these words. All the *people whose names are found in the Book of Life will avoid spiritual Death.* This statement is *for a specific time,* which comes later.

<u>Verse 2</u> confirms the Dead will rise, some to *everlasting life*, and some to *everlasting contempt.* These words can only be valid after Jesus' 1,000-year Kingdom and after God destroys all of Satan's Army at War #2. Therefore, God is laying the foundation for future scriptures. The words are referencing the First and Second Harvests (Rev. 14).

In <u>verse 3</u> is one of the most wonderful messages from God to his children.

Daniel 12:3 *"And they that be wise shall shine as the brightness of the firmament; and they that turn many to righteousness as the stars for ever and ever."*

Verse 4 makes a prophetic statement that can be overlooked. So let us investigate Verse 4.

Daniel 12:4 *"But thou, O Daniel, shut up the words, and seal the book,* even *to the* ___time of the end: many shall run to and fro, and knowledge shall be increased."___

This prophecy reveals the time this prophecy will be exposed to Christians. It has two clues shown here, 1) travel increase and 2) knowledge increased.

We are now traveling anywhere by air, car, spaceship, and train, even to the moon. And the computer is increasing our knowledge by removing God's curse of confused languages. Pay close attention to the words, *"time of the end."* **These words are pertaining to the end of God's plan for humanity.**

Verse 5 This verse does not seem to be, too, important. But all scripture has information.

Daniel 12:5 *"Then I Daniel looked, and, behold, there stood other two, the one on this side of the bank of the river, and the other on that side of the bank of the river."*

There is a curious statement here, why does Daniel identify the *"other two"* as man / woman, angels or a creature? This verse does not fit verse 4 in context with verse 5. But it is related to verse 4 at verse 7 as both verses relate to the last 3½ years of the Great Tribulation, *"where all these things shall be finished."*

So, who are these other two? They are the two witnesses from the first 3½ years of the Great Tribulation. However, these witnesses have not been born yet. Therefore, these verses are about the future of the earth.

Daniel was written in 603 BC, well before the Great Tribulation. One of these witnesses speaks to a man clothed in linen upon the river not in but upon the waters. Who is this third person?

Who has walked on water? Jesus. Notice this man is clothed in linen. It is not referred as white linen. But linen is naturally light in color. White linen is referred to as the future *"righteous acts of the Saints."*

Verse 6, One witness asks a question, *"how long shall it be to the end of these wonders?"* This event is last to reveal when and what will be the sign of the end. *Now specific activities must come to light.* But Daniel is told to seal up this prophecy in verse 9, *"until the time of the end."*.

Verse 7 reveals a man standing on waters (people, tongues, and nations) who swear by God who gives this information for 3½ years for all things to conclude. Here again, *a specific time is given* to us to decipher. And it is found by comparing *in Rev.12:6 to verse 14; 1260 days is equal to 3½ years in the lunar Calendar. These words reveal the last half of the seven years of tribulation.* Proved by *"scatter the power of the holy people."*

This scattering is when Israel escapes into the wilderness (Rev.12:6). And again, Daniel asks, *"what shall be the end of these things."* God identifies these up-and-coming events but *with verses to nail down the specific times.* These times given will pinpoint the very day of Jesus' final 3rd Return to claim back earth and set up His Kingdom of 1,000 years.

Verse 11 gives us the anchor point from which to measure the times for these future events. *This anchor is set at the time the abomination is set up in the rebuilt Jewish Temple.*

There are two events clues spoken of here,

1. **The removal of the Jewish twice a daily sacrifice.**
2. **The abomination set up in the Temple's place for God.**

These two events occur after <u>the first 1260 (3½ years)</u>. It is then the Antichrist #2 (Satan) breaks the seven-year covenant with Israel. Next, you will read this abomination is set up in God's rebuilt Temple in Jerusalem. This event will be last for 1290 days (last 3½ years). This period is the time the abomination is erected and required to be worshiped in the Temple. The 1290 days space pertain to Jesus 3 Return to destroy all evil on earth. But verse 12 adds another event *from the abomination set up in the Temple.*

There you read of 1335 days, which is the time for the Temple cleansing, and Jesus earthly Kingdom begins. These 45 days pertain to,

1. Armageddon War #1. (Jesus verses Satan).
2. Cleansing the war zone. (Seven months to bury the dead).
3. Cleansing the Temple of God.
4. Establish Jesus' government over all the earth.

The Raptured Christians have protection from these coming events of God's wrath.

John 14:1–3 *"(1) Let not your heart be troubled: ye believe in God, believe also in me. (2) In my Father's house are many mansions: if it were not so, I would have told you. I go to prepare a place for you. (3) And if I go and prepare a place for you, I will come again, and receive you unto myself; that where I am, there ye may also be."*

Notice <u>verse 1</u>, Jesus is speaking to the Israelites, who have only believed In God and not Jesus, But Jesus is God, also. But they worship God only as they have been blinded by God. Does this sound convoluted?

Jesus is God so the Jews have unknowingly worshipped Jesus. But it is imperative they worship Jesus for salvation. And by the 144,000, Jesus' Gospel will be preached to the Hebrews during the Great Tribulation

God's ways are not our ways, but John tells us to be at peace for God is in control.

John 14:27 *"Peace I leave with you, my peace I give unto you: not as the world giveth, give I unto you. Let not your heart be troubled, neither let it be afraid."*

Now Jesus speaks to both Hebrew and Christians. But especially to the converted Hebrew converts to Jesus. When you repent and claim Jesus as your Lord and Savior, your saved, and your eternal home is safe from the world events. If you also do the deeds Jesus commands, you will obtain the Great Tribulation. Those (Jew and Gentile) that have accepted Jesus before the Rapture will be spared the wrath of God. And you are a spectator of the end events of earth's evil before the 1,000-year Kingdom of Jesus.

But in the final course of God's plan for man, Christians will be given the mind of Christ. Then we shall know FULLY. Also, keep in mind Rom.8:18.

Romans 8:18, *"For I reckon that the suffering of this present time are not worthy to be compared with the glory which shall be revealed in us."*

This verse is short but contains a powerful message for believers. What God has in mind for us is impossible for us to grasp in our present condition. But we will be glorified, what does glorify truly infer?

From "4888 **soon-daz-ad'-zo**: from *4862* and *1392*:to *exalt* to dignity in company (i.e., similarly) *with:* – glorify together[1]."

From 1392 "**dox'-ah;** from the base of *1380; glory* (as very *apparent),* to a wide application (lit. or fig., obj. Or subj): –dignity, glory, (-ious), honor, praise, worship[1]."

Most of us Christians cannot grasp this glory to be revealed in us. Those that been exceedingly successful in sports or entertainments, may have some idea of earthly glory.

Notice the words very apparent, dignity, honor, praise, worship, are words most individuals have never experienced. Exceptions are high school or college graduation. But these will not come close to the glory God will give Christians.

We cannot understand, nor will words reveal the magnitude of this word Glory. You will be special in God's and Jesus' Kingdom. Everything will be available to you. All hurtful memories will disappear, health will be perfect, no mental, no physical, no fear, no nervousness, no strangers, no restriction, no lust of the flesh or eyes, perfect surrounding, and most of all LOVE.

We have never experienced perfection so how can we tell of it?

Believers

My Christian brother and sisters do not miss the Rapture. Wake up as Jesus will come as a thief in the night and those brothers and sister who are not working for Jesus' Kingdom will be left behind. Do not deceive yourself with incomplete knowledge about the requirements for the Rapture. Works or Deeds have always been a part of God's plan.

Non-believers

For you who have not repented and baptized into Jesus; please give Jesus' salvation thoughtful consideration. Study the ramification, truths in the Bibles, ask Jesus to come into your life. Remember you are only going to be on earth for 70 the 80 years, and then comes eternity.

Do not fall for Satan deceptions of when it is over it over, That is a wish he concocted to fool unwary individuals who want their self-will fulfilled. Life after death is a proven event by science. There are many false concepts you have been taught in school of higher learning, which come from Satan's trap. It is <u>extremely important that **you** study for the truth</u>. One great item to study is the Bible.

Daniel's prophecies spoken of here was circa 607 BC to today is 2022 AD that makes prophecy 2629 years old: 644 years before Jesus, mission on earth

✝

❧ CHAPTER 16 ❧

The Rapture

The Rapture is not a parable in itself but is the product of a number of parables mentioned in the Bible. And I am trying to bring these parables into sequence leading to the end times. As building blocks, they must be introduced as the product of the framework of our house. Each room must be framed in its time before the roof can be started. And the interior cannot be finished until the roof is finished. Thereby, waterproofing the interior for its completion.

The roofing is a metaphor for the protection of our hearts. In the plan of God, our change of our heart from correction to in correction is protected by the completed house. Exterior, what light we are to reflect of Jesus, and the interior (Knowledge, Love, obedience, and the character, and mind of Jesus) is a special and sensitive time.

Jesus revealed this when He arose for the grave and Mary Magdalene wanted to touch Jesus. But Jesus said to her, *"Touch me not: for I have not ascended to the Father."*(Joh.20:17) Have you ever wonder what this means?

This is that transition from corruption to incorruption. Jesus was corrupted when He took on himself the sins of all humanity. Why the do not to touched is unknown at the time, but it has meaning for this transition.

CHRISTIANS ARE NOT APPOINTED TO GOD'S WRATH

In God's plan for man, He revealed that for humankind to be with God in His present, an individuals must be perfect. But perfect in what? This information was not revealed to Adam and Eve. Why? It was not until scriptures were written later; this condition is revealed to man, through the blood of Jesus.

And it is through this blood that believers in God's son, that we become a perfect individual. Therefore, all believers will be perfect, and we can be with God eternally.

Therefore, God cannot chastise the perfect individual, this would not be perfection from God. So, God devised a way to remove the perfect form the Great Tribulation. It is called the Rapture. There God removes the righteous dead and alive Saints to paradise in Heaven with Him and Jesus. This is a Passover for all the righteous. They will have gone through the corruption to incorruption phase. We have been given the mind of Christ and are spectors to the coming events.

However, God has some lazy believers. So. what is God to do to motivate these lazy into action? *God creates the last chance for salvation to motivate the lazy and convert, The Jews to their Messiah, Jesus.* So, what is this period of motivation? It is called The Great Tribulation. It is designed to place the lazy, the Israelites, and border line believers, into an obvious situation and last chance to be with God forever. It is revealed in the Valley of Decision.

Last or final chance for humans' salvation. This is where God is chastising his children. It is a period of seven years remaining from Israel's 490 Years of refusing to come to Jesus, their Messiah. God's wrath will be so terrible that if Jesus does not return, no life will survive. However, Jesus does return and is shown in many scriptures. The best Scripture for his return is found Rev, 19

This chapter is dedicated to War #1 Armageddon, which comes at the end of the Great Tribulation. This is Jesus' 3rd Return to earth to destroy all evil individuals. This is the beginning of Jesus' 1,000-year Kingdom.

Jesus' city for His capital will be Jerusalem. It is there that the worlds' nation will come to praise and worship Jesus. This is the time all the Church Saints will rule with Jesus.

There will be no evil in the beginning of Jesus' Kingdom. However, the righteous survivors of War#1 will still have the Sin nature given to Christians by Adam. And their children will have it, too. Some of these children will not accept Jesus as their king. It is these evil children who will not be allowed into Jesus' city Jerusalem. It is this rejection and shame that will cause the weeping and gnashing of teeth.

Satan's covert disobedience continues in man during a wonderful time on earth. This is God's way to prove to Christians it is not Satan that will tempt us but ourselves by the lust of the eyes and lust of the flesh.

CHAPTER 17

Jesus' 3rd Return

Armageddon

Again, I am including a subject which is not a parable in itself but is revealed by other parables. This is God way to show the usefulness of parables to clarify other scriptures. And you will find the next paragraph become clearer with its position after War#1, Armageddon.

First, I would you look at the Old Testament prophecies relating to War #1. And one is found in the book of Ezekiel Chapter 39. From the chapter forward is future to Israel. I will shorten the verses of Chapter 39 to the point of Armageddon.

Ezekiel 39:7–12 "(7) *So will I make <u>my holy name known in the midst of my people Israel;</u> and I will not* let them *pollute my holy name any more: and the heathen shall know that I* am *the LORD, the Holy One in Israel. (8) Behold, it is come, and it is done, saith the Lord GOD; this* is *the day whereof I have spoken. (9) And they that dwell in the cities of <u>Israel shall go forth, and shall set on fire and burn the weapons, both the shields and the bucklers, the bows and the arrows, and the hand staves, and the spears, and they shall burn them with fire seven years:</u> (10) So that they shall take no wood out of the field, neither cut down* any *out of the forests; for they shall burn the weapons with fire: and they shall spoil those that* *spoiled them, and rob those that robbed them, saith the Lord GOD. (11) And it shall come to pass in that day,* that *I will give <u>unto Gog a place there of graves in Israel</u>, the valley of the passengers on the east of the sea: and it shall stop the noses of the passengers: and there shall they bury Gog and all his multitude: and they shall call it The valley of Hamongog. (12) And seven months shall the house of Israel be burying of them, that they may cleanse the land.*

In <u>verse 7</u> you will read the name of Jesus will be known by Israel. This means Jesus is known as the son of God, Israel's Messiah and His name will never be polluted any more. This can only happen after War #1. Then is when Jesus' 1,000-year Kingdom begins.

Joel Chapters 2–3 also reveals this war #1. Also in Micah 4:1–7 you will read of Jesus coming to earth.

Revelation 19 Is all about War #1 Armageddon. And in verses 7–9 is

Speaking to the Marriage of Jesus to His Bride the Church, which follows in Chapter 20.

Here are some parables which point to Jesus' Returns.

1. The Hidden Treasure.---Mat. 13:44.
2. The valuable pearl. ---Mat,13:45–46.
3. The Wheat and the Tares.--- Mat.1313:24–30
4. The Lost Sheep.---Mat. 18:12–14
5. The Wedding Feast. --- Mat. 22:2–14
6. The Ten Virgins.---Mat. 25:1–13
7. Sheep and Goats.---Mat 25:31–46
8. Many Prophecies also add to both returns of Jesus.

I hope you see the application these parables apply for clarification for other scripture, too.

Without the knowledge of the Book of Revelation, many concepts or doctrines will not be correctly understood. Case on point is the understanding of the final destination of lost souls. It is not Hell but the Lake of Fire. (Rev.20:14–15)

Another point is the salvation of the Israelites through the Gospel of Jesus to the Jews during the Great Tribulation. I have never heard a pastor preach a sermon on this subject as if the Jews, God's elect, do not matter.

I also have never heard a sermon on the Last Chance for Salvation revealed in Revelation. Why is it Christianity does not teach the full Gospel of Jesus Christ by avoiding Revelation. It is teachers and preachers not teaching this book are subject to God curse in Rev.22.

Revelation 22:18–19 *"(18) For I testify unto every man that heareth the words of the prophecy of this book, If any man shall add unto these things, God shall add unto him the plagues that are written in this book: (19 And if any man shall take away from the words of the book of this prophecy, God shall take away his part out of the book of life, and out of the holy city, and from the things which are written in this book.*

How could anyone not teach and preach this book? I have heard, it is because *it does not have the Gospel revealed in this book.* How wrong can the seminaries be using this excuse. If this is the case, why do they teach the Old Testament in detail.

Some Christians believe these verses pertain to the complete Bible. However, John did not have the completed scriptures with him on Patmos, where he wrote Revelation. Therefore, these verses pertain to the Book he wrote there on that island.

In your prayer life, add in our brother and sisters Jews, that they accept Jesus as their Messiah now, today. As there must be 144,000 Hebrews missionaries knowledgeable of Jesus Gospel during the Great Tribulation to convert the Jews to Jesus as their Messiah. If this is not a major event of the Gospel being mentioned, then what is?

Remember 1st John 4, where we are to test all spirits giving us information. That means we have some homework to do! This s especially true in Faith and Deeds.

You have heard, you cannot work yourself into salvation. *Well, that is half true.* This is true for Christians before the Rapture, but after the Rapture, the deed of not accepting the Mark of the Beast, is a deed you must perform thereby, working yourself in Heaven, Salvation.

❧ CHAPTER 18 ❦

The Gnashing of Teeth

Mat. 8:12

Matthew 8:11–12 "(11) And *I say unto you, that many shall come from the east and west and shall sit down with Abraham, and Isaac, and Jacob, in the kingdom of heaven. (12) But the children of the kingdom shall be cast out into outer darkness: there shall be weeping and gnashing of teeth.*"

Verse 11 is spoken of in several verses of this occurrence, and I am starting with this one. The first *clue* is many will come, but it is not clear in itself. But the clarity depends on the *2ⁿᵈ clue, which* is in the kingdom of Heaven, and the *3ʳᵈ clue* is they will set down with Abraham, Isaac, and Jacob.

Being these men are Old Testament Saints, it is clear this event is after the 1ˢᵗ Harvest (to be in Heaven), and before Jesus' earthly 1,000-year Kingdom. It also reveals these men have died. Being in Heaven shows these men are righteous (saved) of the *Old Testament Saints.*

Verse 12 However, puts a twist on this meaning as we read of the event in the *clue,* "*the children of the kingdom shall be cast out into outer darkness: there shall be weeping and gnashing of teeth.*"

This statement requires us to have some understanding of future events. Many of us were taught this *"weeping and gnashing"* referrers to Hell (place of Torment), *but this is partly true.* Hell is an English word for many separate locations for punishment. But it is not the final destination for the lost; that name is the Lake of Fire Rev.20:14–15.

There you will read in the King James Bible that death and Hell are cast into the Lake of Fire. Here is where *the traditions of our final destination have been confus*ed. I do not believe anyone in the Lake of Fire will be weeping or gnashing their teeth but screaming. So, there is another place of punishment before the Lake of Fire.

In Luk.16, we read the parable of Lazarus and the rich man. There, Lazarus was a poor beggar full of sores lay at his gate. The rich man never helped Lazarus at all, not a crumb from his table. Both died, and Lazarus was in heaven in the bosom of Abraham, and the rich man was in a place I call Torments (Hell).

The rich man asked Abraham to send Lazarus with a drop of water to cool his tongue. But there was a rift between Heaven and Hell (Torment) that no one could cross. This parable reveals much, but I want you to see these two distinct locations, Heaven and Hell, for now. But Torments captures the concept best. As I see, Hell, as a holding point, enroute to the Lake of Fire. Hell is there that all lost souls are kept until the Great White Throne Judgment of God's for all lost souls.

Note

This location is not Purgatory to pay for sins; for only Jesus, death can pay the sin debt. And if you are in Jesus, your sin debt is paid But if you are not in Jesus, your sin debt can never be paid.

It seems redundant to send them to the Lake of Fire and bring them back to be judged and sent back to the Lake of Fire. Therefore, in Mat.8:12,

Jesus is referring to the place of Torment. What better punishment for the lost souls to feel the heat from the Lake of Fire and see their final destination before the Great White Throne Judgment.

So, who are these mentioned in verse 12? Who are these children outside the kingdom? These are those Children of those who are alive during Jesus' 1,000-year Kingdom. They are born to the mortal Tribulation Saints who survived the Great Tribulation. Many of these children grow into adults and are still disobedient to the King (Jesus). Sin will be present in Jesus' earthly Kingdom due to the *Tribulation Saints survivor of Armageddon.* They still carry the sin nature given by Adam.

These children mention here will be Satan Army collected at the end of Jesus 1,000 Kingdom. Satan will recruit these children after his release from the abyss Rev.20:7—9. But God destroys this army. This event is the 2nd Harvest of Rev.14:17—20. Then comes the final judgment for all lost souls, The Great White Throne Judgment in Rev. 20:10–15.

Note

For years, I was taught that the 2nd Harvest period was based on the _clue_ revealed in verse 20, as it was the extension of Exe.39:11–15. However, the _evidence_ in Rev.14:13 of *"the temple in heaven"* reveals the temple is not on earth. Therefore, the New Earth has not been created yet (Rev.21:3), and God's Temple is not on earth until after the New Earth.

Now there could be some problem here as the verse in Rev.14:17 uses the *Temple,* where the verse in Rev.21 uses Tabernacle's word. The first use of tabernacle was back in Moses' days during the exodus from Egypt (sin). God gave Moses the Tabernacle's construction data, which was the place God would lead Israel through the desert.

The Temple is a permanent place of worship, and the Tabernacle is transit Holy place of leading and worship. The Tabernacle in Rev.21:3 will be a place; God will lead us into eternity. Also, these words can mean the same location. The Temple is the same as the Tabernacle, for we are to worship the Triune God, and we are to be led by the Triune God.

Another event we read about the weeping and gnashing of teeth is in Mat.24:46–51; we see *clues* about the servants of Jesus.

Matthew 24:46–51 "(46) *Blessed* **is that servant, whom his lord** *when he cometh shall find so doing. (47)Verily I say unto you, That he shall make him ruler over all his goods. (48) But and if that evil servant shall say in his heart, My lord delayeth his coming; (49) And shall begin to* smite **his fellowservants, and to eat and drink with the drunken;** *(50) The lord of that servant shall come in a day when he looketh not for* **him,** *and in an hour that he is not aware of, (51) And shall cut him asunder, and appoint* **him his portion with the hypocrites:** *there shall be weeping and gnashing of teeth."*

This scripture comes at the end of the ten virgins' chapter, where five prepared for Jesus (Bridegroom) and five not prepared. The unprepared were left behind. These words are speaking of the Rapture. It is evident in scripture there those who are of faith but without deeds will be left behind to go through the Great Tribulation. I call them the *Tribulation Saints.* They are saved by faith but are without deeds for Jesus' Kingdom.

Notice the *clue* "*when he comes shall find so doing."* Is this not clear that we are the servants continuing doing until he comes? Notice the *clue* of the doing servant's reward, is ruling.

Now compare the results of the evil servant ignoring Jesus' command to go into all nations and the basic beatitudes of Christians. Another important *clue* is, Jesus *comes at a time the unworthy servant is unaware.* This time is *the thief in the night.*

Jesus has warned us about this coming many times in the scriptures. We are told in many places to be watching for Jesus' return, and how can we know the approximate time of his arrival if we do not study the Bible? This is the time of the Rapture and those left behind.

Again, the left behind will be in the Great Tribulation, where there will be a weeping (sorry they missed the Rapture) and gnashing of teeth due to the anguish they will experience here during the rule of Satan on earth. Here again, are the *Tribulation Saints* saved by faith but without deeds.

The last verse (51), I want you to read, is where Jesus is speaking of the time on his final 3rd Return to earth. Jesus will destroy all evil in War #1 of Armageddon and then set up his 1,000 years earthly Kingdom. I want you to see the consistency of the fate of the Tribulation Saints and the faithfulness of God and Jesus.

Matthew 25:30—34 "(30) And *cast ye the unprofitable servant into outer darkness: there shall be weeping and gnashing of teeth.* (31) When the Son of man shall come in his glory, and all the holy angels with him, then shall he sit upon the throne of his glory: (32) And before him shall be gathered all nations: and he shall <u>separate</u> them one from another, as a shepherd divideth his *sheep from the goats:* (33) And he shall set <u>the sheep on his right hand, but the goats on the left.</u> (34) Then shall the King say unto them on his right hand, Come, ye blessed of my Father, <u>inherit the kingdom</u> prepared for you from the foundation of the world:"

These complete verses continue with information for your edification and recommend your study of them. But for the *Tribulation Saints* is " *the weeping and gnashing of teeth,*" I plan to stop here in verse 34.

<u>Verse 30</u> is the end of the dissertation of the unprofitable servant. If you go back and read the verses, you will see this servant given a talent to invest for his master to make a profit. However, he just buried it

Now, does this not appear as many Christians today? God has given every one of us at least one talent, and we are to find that talent and put it into use in Jesus' Kingdom. To do less is just *burying our talent*, doing nothing for Jesus (Master).

This burying is reflective of the Pew Sitters in the Church today. They have faith and come and worship but do nothing for the advancement of Christianity. These Pew Sitters will be left behind to face the Great Tribulation. Now there seems to be a change of thought to the verses following.

How do you think the weak and deedless will react to being left behind? Confused, why me, God is not real, I hate God, He has lied to me, and other feeling of abandonment. God has given us warnings and clues which lazy Christians are unknowledge of these clues. But many (I hope) will research the Bible and find the reason they were left behind. They have not been taught by teachers and Pastors the Book of Revelation. They have been sweet and pleasant words of Love and comfort, And not the tough words of hard Love, truths.

Note

No messages of Hell Fire and Brimstone is taught anymore. Religious Collages, seminaries have all but removed the Book of Revelation from the curriculum. I have heard told that there is no Gospel in it therefore, small attention is given to it. How can religious institutions of learning not teach this book in details? Revelation is full of the Gospel of Jesus. The 144,000 Jewish Missionaries will teach and convert the Jews to Jesus by His Gospel. Where do this 144,000 get their knowledge of the Gospel? For years they have rejected Jesus as their Messiah. But God reveals they have a powerful Gospel proven by the fact they convert all Jews to Jesus during the Great Tribulation

Verse 31 changes the timing to Jesus' future 2nd Return because the throne of his glory is speaking of his throne in his 1,000-year Kingdom. But further investigation appears to be speaking of the Rapture.

In Rev. 14:14, this can be Jesus on his glory on a white cloud with his crown to harvest righteous souls. I see the 1st Harvest mentioned here as the righteous souls (Old Testament Saints and Tribulation Saints) are from every nation.

The 2nd Harvest is the souls captured in the great winepress of God. These are those who rebelled against Jesus during His 1,000-year Kingdom. They are collected at death and War#2.

Verse 32 speaks of the gathering of all nations. This verse further identifies the gathering of Jesus' sheep and Goats. One thing to keep in mind is that goats were approved sacrificial animals, as were the sheep. *Then the separation of sheep and goats is the separation of approved sacrifices.* So, what are the differences? Sheep are relatively obedient animals, as goats are more difficult animals to lead. So, this is the separation between obedient Christians and Pew Sitters.

Verse 33 reveals the sheep are on the right hand (hand of honor) and goats on the left. The sheep are honored because they have maintained the faith and performed a deed to advance Jesus' kingdom.

This stems from most people who are right-handed. It is an insult even today to touch someone or eat food in the desert countries with your left hand.

The Goats can take on the sheep's reward during the Great Tribulation by rejecting the Mark of the Beast and thereby, become sheep by doing this deed while remaining faithful to Jesus.

This concept is supported in the parable of the Wheat and the Tares in Mat.13:24–30. It would seem appropriate for the *faithful Tribulation Saints, who go through God's Great Tribulation and now do the deeds while remaining faithful,* will prove themselves worthy of Jesus' Kingdom and salvation. Therefore, the Goats have made themselves clean and surrogate sheep, now called Wheat. This event is the 1st Harvest (Rev.14) and is of righteous souls of the dead Old Testament Saints and dead Tribulation Saints.

This 1st Harvest is the collection of righteous dead souls from after the Rapture to the end of Armageddon. We must now jump ahead to see the results of deeds versus lack of deeds.

Verses 45 and 46 reveal the do-nothing (did not's) for Jesus' kingdom individuals. Please read the verses between the deeds of Wheat (surrogate sheep) as opposed to the Tares that have done nothing for Jesus. War #2 starts after War #1 and is the collection of lost souls who die in Jesus' 1,000-year Kingdom.

God will destroy all evil individuals from Jesus' Kingdom. War #2's' collection of the dead lost souls begins after War #1 and ends after Jesus' 1,000-year Kingdom.

They are sent to Torment to wait for the Great White Throne Judgment of God and then sent to the Lake of Fire.

Next, the Wheat (surrogate sheep) shall go into eternal life. Notice no mention of rulership; therefore, these are the *Tribulation Saints.* Except for the 144,000 Hebrew missionaries of Rev.7, they will rule with Christ.

With this information, we can deduce that the weeping and gnashing of teeth is different from the Lake of Fire. So, when you read this description of punishment, think of it as pointing to the place I call Torment (Hell) and not the final location in the Lake of Fire.

LESSON LEARNED

1. God has a deed in Heaven for some to comfort newcomers.
2. The alive evil children of Jesus' 1,000-year Kingdom will not be permitted into Jerusalem during Jesus' 1,000-year kingdom.
3. We learn of the separation of the sheep and goats in the Rapture.
4. The Goats repent and do the deeds of Jesus during the Great Tribulation to become righteous Wheat.
5. We see the different movements of good versus evil individuals.

   a. The *faithful and doers* are taken to Heaven in the *Rapture.*
   b. The *Tribulation Saints now do the deeds* required for salvation. They are removed just before War #1 (Armageddon) in the 1st Harvest.
   c. The *evil children born during Jesus' 1,000-year Kingdom* will not be permitted into Jerusalem during those 1,000 years. This restriction is the *cause of the "weeping and gnashing of teeth."*
   d. These evil children will eventually join Satan and be destroyed in the 2nd Harvest (War #2) by God. All evil will be sent to the Lake of Fire.

6. There is a place of punishment (Torments) before the Lake of Fire.

Additional information on Hell.

Hell is English for the various places spoken of in Hebrew and Greek languages. Those languages use more words to describe distinct items. We have the same problem with the word love. In Greek, there are different words for diverse types of love. Agape is Godly love; another is for the brotherly kind of love; another is for a charitable type of love and many more. In English, they just used Love. And it is so with Hell.

A few names are used for *"the place of the dead," "the grave,"* and others, including the *righteous* and the *unrighteous dead* souls. But there are two (2) specific names for the unrighteous dead. The two I have found are called *"place of torment" or "Hell."* In all the cases above, the word Hell is used in the English language exclusively. This usage is very misleading to English-speaking peoples. There is *no single word in Greek* to explain the final eternal destination for the unrighteous. *Therefore, the King James calls the* place of everlasting punishment **"the Lake of Fire**." So, it would appear that the location of *Torment* (Hell) is a lesser punishment holding place, which is before the maximum punishment place called,

The LAKE OF FIRE.

CHAPTER 19

Cast Out's from Jesus' Kingdom

Matthew 8:11–12 "(11) And *I say unto you, That many shall come from the east and west and shall sit down with Abraham, and Isaac, and Jacob, in the kingdom of heaven. (12) But the children of the kingdom shall be cast out into outer darkness: there shall be weeping and gnashing of teeth."*

Several verses speak of this occurrence, and I am starting with this one. The first _clue_ is many will come, but it is not clear in itself. But the clarity depends on the _2ⁿᵈ clue_ in the kingdom of Heaven, and the _3ʳᵈ clue_ is they will set down with Abraham, Isaac, and Jacob. Being these men are in the Kingdom in Heaven and not on earth, it is clear this event is before Jesus' earthly 1,000-year Kingdom. It also reveals these men have died. Being in Heaven shows these men are righteous (saved) of the *Old Testament Saints*

Note

In the original Bible there was no chapter and verse. So, I want you to read verses 11–12 without using the number and you will see that the Kingdom in Heaven is different than the kingdom. In verse 12 is Jesus' earthly kingdom of 1,000 years.

Verse 12 puts a twist on this meaning as we read of the event in the _clue_, "*the children of the kingdom shall be cast out into outer darkness:*

there shall be weeping and gnashing of teeth." This statement requires us to have some understanding of future events.

Many of us were taught this *"weeping and gnashing"* referrers to Hell (place of Torment), *but this is partly true.* Hell is an English word used for many separate locations for punishment. But it is not the final destination for the lost; that name is the Lake of Fire, Rev.20:15.

There you will read in the King James Bible that death and Hell are cast into the Lake of Fire. Here is where *the traditions of our final destination have been confus*ed. I do not believe anyone in the Lake of Fire will be weeping or gnashing their teeth but screaming. So, there is another place of punishment before the Lake of Fire.

In Luk.16, we read the parable of Lazarus and the rich man. There, Lazarus was a poor beggar full of sores lay at his gate. The rich never helped Lazarus at all, not a crumb from his table. Both died, and Lazarus was in heaven in the bosom of Abraham, and the rich man was in a place I call Torments (Hell). The rich man asked Abraham to send Lazarus with a drop of water to cool his tongue. But there was a rift between Heaven and Hell (Torment) that no one could cross.

This parable reveals much, but for now, I want you to see these two distinct locations, Heaven and Hell. But Torments captures the concept best. Hell, as a holding point, is en route to the Lake of Fire. It is there that all lost souls are stored until the Great White Throne of God's judgment for all lost souls.

Note

This location is not Purgatory to pay for sins; for only Jesus, death can pay the sin debt. And if you are in Jesus, your sin debt is paid. But if you are not in Jesus, your sin debt can never be paid.

It seems redundant to send them to the Lake of Fire (Hell) and bring them back to be judged and sent to the Lake of Fire. Therefore, in Mat.8:12, Jesus is referring to the place of Torment; what better punishment for the lost souls to feel the heat from the Lake of Fire and see their destination before the Great White Throne Judgment.

So, who are these mentioned in verse 12? Who are these children outside the kingdom? These are those children of those who are alive during Jesus' 1,000-year Kingdom who are born to the mortal Tribulation Saints who survived the Great Tribulation.

These children grow into adults, and some are disobedient to the King (Jesus). Sin will be present in Jesus' Kingdom due to the *Tribulation Saints survivor of Armageddon*. They still carry the sin nature given to Adam.

These children mention here will be Satan's Army collected at the end of Jesus' 1,000-year Kingdom. Satan will recruit these children after his release from the abyss Rev.20:7–9. But God destroys this army. This destruction is at the end of the 2nd Harvest of Rev.14:17–20. Then comes the final judgment for all lost souls, The Great White Throne Judgment in Rev. 20:10—15.

Note

For years, I was taught that the 2nd Harvest period was based on the *clue* revealed in verse 20, as it was the extension of Exe.39:11–15. However, the *clue* in Rev.14:13 of *"the temple in heaven"* reveals the Temple is not on earth. Therefore, the New Earth has not been created yet (Rev.21:3), and God's Temple is not on earth until after the creation of the New Earth.

There could be a problem here as the verse in Rev.14:17 uses the *Temple*, where the verse in Rev.21 uses the word *Tabernacle*. Tabernacle's first use was back in Moses' days during the exodus from Egypt (sin). God gave Moses the construction data for the Tabernacle, which was the place God would lead Israel through the desert.

The Temple appears a permanent place of worship, and the Tabernacle is a place of leading us, gypsies. If this is so, then the tabernacle in Rev.21:3 will be a place, God will lead us into eternity. Also, these words can mean the exact location. The Temple is the same as the Tabernacle, for we are to worship the Triune God, and we are to be led by the Triune God.

Another event we read about the weeping and gnashing of teeth is in Mat.24:46–51; we see *clues* about the servants of Jesus.

Matthew 24:46—51 "*(46) Blessed* **is that servant, whom his lord** *when he cometh shall find so doing. (47)Verily I say unto you, That* **he shall make** *him ruler over all his goods.* **(48) But and if that evil** *servant shall say in his heart, My lord delayeth his coming; (49) And* ***shall begin to*** smite **his fellowservants, and to eat and drink with** **the drunken;** *(50) The lord of that servant shall come in a day when* *he looketh not for* **him,** *and in an hour that he is not aware of, (51)* *And shall cut him asunder, and appoint* **him** **his portion with the** **hypocrites:** *there shall be weeping and gnashing of teeth.*"

This scripture comes at the end of the chapter of the ten virgins, where five were prepared for Jesus (Bridegroom), and five were not prepared. The unprepared were left behind. This event is speaking of the Rapture. It is evident in scripture that those of faith but without deeds will be left behind to go through the Great Tribulation. I call them the *Tribulation Saints.* They are saved by faith but are without deeds for Jesus' Kingdom.

Notice the *clue* "*when he comes shall find so doing.*" Is this not clear that we the servants are to continue doing until he comes? Notice the *clue* of the doing servant's reward, ruling. Now compare the results of the evil servant ignoring Jesus' command to go into all nations and the basic beatitudes of Christians.

Another important _clue_ is, Jesus *comes at a time the unworthy servant is unaware.* This coming is the thief in the night Jesus has warned us about many times in the scriptures. We are told in many places to be watching for Jesus' return, and how can we know the approximate time of his arrival if we do not study the Bible? This period is the time of the Rapture and those left behind.

Again, they will be in the Great Tribulation, where there will be a weeping (sorry they missed the Rapture) and gnashing of teeth due to the anguish they will experience here during the rule of Satan on earth. Here again, are the *Tribulation Saints* saved by faith but no deeds.

The last verse (Mat.24:51, please read, is where Jesus is speaking of the time on his final 3rd Return to earth, but so is Mat.25:30–34. Jesus will destroy all evil in War #1 of Armageddon and then set up His 1,000-year earthly kingdom. I want you to see the consistency of the Tribulation Saints' fate and the faithfulness of God and Jesus.

Matthew 25:30—34 *"(30) And <u>cast ye the unprofitable servant into outer darkness: there shall be weeping and gnashing of teeth.</u> (31) <u>When the Son of man shall come in his glory,</u> and all the holy angels with him, then shall he sit upon the throne of his glory: (32) And before him shall be gathered all nations: and he shall <u>separate</u> them one from another, as a shepherd divideth his *sheep from the goats: (33) And he shall set <u>the sheep on his right hand, but the goats on the left.</u> (34) Then shall the King say unto them on his right hand, Come, ye blessed of my Father, <u>inherit the kingdom</u> prepared for you from the foundation of the world:"*

Notice the underlined words, *"when the Son of man shall come,* which is Jesus' 3rd Return. Also, *"inherit the kingdom,"* is when the Church Saints inherit from God. Notice that this event God has planned for before creation. Those killed by Jesus go to Torment (Hell), this is the "outer darkness:" This is the place of *"weeping and gnashing of teeth."*

Verse 30 is the end of the dissertation of the unprofitable servant. If you go back and read the verses, you will see this servant given one talent to invest for his master to make a profit. However, he just buried it. Now, does this not appear as many Christians today?

God has given every one of us at least one talent (ability), and we are to find that talent and put it into use in Jesus' Kingdom. To do less is just burying our talent, doing nothing for Jesus (Master). This burying is reflective of the Pew Sitters in the Church today. They have faith and come and worship but do nothing for the advancement of Christianity. These Pew Sitters will be left behind to face the Great Tribulation. This, too, is mainly when there will be weeping and gnashing of teeth.

Verse 31 reveals the time of His 3rd Return. As the throne of his glory appears to be speaking of his throne in his earthly kingdom. In Rev.14:14, this can be Jesus on *"his throne in glory"* on a white cloud with his crown to perform the 1st Harvest of righteous souls. The 2nd Harvest is the souls captured in the great winepress of God. I see the 1st Harvest mentioned here as the righteous souls (Old Testament Saints and Tribulation Saints) from all nations, but the 2nd Harvest is for all lost souls.

Verse 32 speaks of the gathering of all nations. This gathering further identifies the collection of Jesus' sheep and Goats. Notice the words "a Shepherd divideth." And Jesus is our shepherd. One thing to keep in mind is that goats were approved sacrificial animals, as were the sheep. *Then the separation of sheep and goats is the separation of approved sacrifices.* So, what are the differences? Sheep are relatively obedient animals, as goats are more difficult animals to lead. This is the separation between obedient Christians and Pew Sitters.

<u>Verse 33</u> reveals the sheep are placed on the right hand (hand of honor) and goats on the left. The sheep honored because they have maintained the faith and performed a deed to advance Jesus' kingdom.

The right hand is the hand of honor. It stems from most people who are right-handed. It is an insult even today to touch someone or eat food in desert countries with your left hand.

The Goats can take on the sheep's reward during the Great Tribulation by rejecting the Mark of the Beast and thereby, become sheep by not accepting the Mark while remaining faithful to Jesus.

This concept is supported in the parable of the Wheat and the Tares in Mat.13:24–30. It would seem appropriate for the *faithful Tribulation Saints* who go through God's Great Tribulation and do the deeds. And remain faithful to prove themselves worthy of Jesus' kingdom and salvation.

Therefore, the Goats have worked to make themselves clean and are surrogate sheep called Wheat. This occurrence is the 1st Harvest (Rev.14) and is of righteous souls of the dead Old Testament Saints and dead Tribulation Saints.

> We must now jump ahead to see the results of these two Saints' deeds versus lack of deeds.

Matthew 25:46–47 "*(44) Then shall they also answer him, saying, Lord, when saw we thee an hungred, or athirst, or a stranger, or naked, or sick, or in prison, and did not minister unto thee? (45) Then shall he answer them, saying, Verily I say unto you, Inasmuch as ye did* it not to one of the least of these, ye did it not to me.

(46) And these shall go away into everlasting punishment: but the righteous into life eternal."

<u>Verses 44–46</u> reveal the results of the do-nothing individuals for Jesus' kingdom. Read these verses between the deeds of the Wheat (surrogate sheep) as opposed to the Tares that have done nothing for Jesus. <u>Verse 46</u> shows the 2nd Harvest of Rev. 14, in which God destroys the deedless in War #2. This destruction is the war where God destroys all evil individuals from Jesus' Kingdom (Rev.20:7–15). They are sent to the Great White Throne Judgment of God then to the Lake of Fire.

Notice in this verse, the destination of the Tares is into everlasting punishment. This destination is not the place of Torment but into the Lake of Fire. And next, the Wheat (surrogate sheep) shall go into eternal life. Notice no mention of rulership; therefore, these are the *Tribulation Saints*. Except for the 144,000 Hebrew missionaries of Rev.7, they will rule with Christ.

With this information, we can deduce that the weeping and gnashing of teeth is different from the Lake of Fire. So, when you read this description of punishment, think of it as pointing to the place I call Torment (Hell), the tribulation period and not the final location in the Lake of Fire.

LESSONS LEARNED

1. God has a deed in Heaven for some to comfort newcomers.
2. The evil children are cast out of Jesus' 1,000-year Kingdom. They will not be permitted into Jerusalem during Jesus' kingdom. The location of Jesus' throne for 1,000 years.
3. We learned of the separation of the sheep and goats in the Rapture.
4. The Goats repent and do the deeds of Jesus during the Great Tribulation to become righteous Wheat.

5. We see the different movements of good versus evil individuals. The *faithful and doers* go to heaven *(Raptured)*.

6. The *Tribulation Saints now do the deeds* required for salvation. They are removed before War #1 Armageddon in the 1st Harvest just before War #1 (Armageddon).

7. The *evil children born during Jesus' 1,000-year Kingdom* will not be permitted into Jerusalem during those 1,000 years, and therefore, the *"weeping and gnashing of teeth."*

8. These evil children will eventually join Satan and be destroyed in the 2nd Harvest (War #2) by God. All evil is sent to the Lake of Fire.

9. There is a place of punishment (Torments) before the Lake of Fire.

Additional information on Hell.

Hell is an English translation for the separate places spoken of in Hebrew and Greek languages. Those languages use more words to describe distinct items. We have the same problem with the word Love. In Greek, there are different words for several types of love. Agape is Godly love; another is for a brotherly kind of love; another is for the charitable kind of love and many more. In English, they just used Love. And it is so with Hell.

Different names are used for *"the place of the dead," "the grave,"* and others, including the *righteous* and *unrighteous* souls. But there are two (2) specific names for the unrighteous dead. The two I have found are called *"place of torment,"* the same as '*Hell,*' and the '*Lake of Fire.*'

In all the cases above, the word Hell is used in the English language. This Hell is very misleading to English-speaking peoples. As far as I know, there is *no single word in Greek* to explain the final eternal destination for the unrighteous. *Therefore, the King James calls the* place of everlasting punishment, *"the Lake of Fire."* You can read where Hell is cast into the *Lake of Fire* in Rev.20:14. This shows that the place of *Torment* is a lesser punishment holding place, which is before maximum punishment place called, **The LAKE OF FIRE.**

What a perfect pipeline for sinners. First to a place of torment where they can feel the intense heat from the Lake of Fire, which they know it is their home forever. If you remember the Parable of the rich man and Lazarus

Before I move on, I want you to realize that The Great Tribulation is the last place for salvation. It will be extremely difficult to accept Jesus as to do so is a death sentence for you or your family. The only people who will be preaching the Gospel will be a 140,000 Jewish missionary scattered around the globe.

And protected by God. But there is no protection for the ½ christians. They will be sought after and killed at will.

Do not delay your efforts in adding to Jesus' Kingdom. Get busy find your talent and put into actions.

CHAPTER 20

The Wedding Feast

Mat. 22:1–13

Matthew 22:2 *"The <u>kingdom of heaven</u> is like unto a certain king, which made a marriage for his son,"*

This parable is a little long and I will hit the highlights. So, look at the kingdom of heaven it is the certain king, God. It is He revealing a marriage for his son Jesus. My question is for what purpose?

Many get marriage for love, to get away from home, for money, for prestige, and/or to have children. Jesus does not need to get away from Heaven, He has no need for money, here is no higher prestige, and He will have all the righteous children. So, there must be some reason.

For an answer we will need more information and it is in this parable.

1. Who is the bride? Notice there is not mention of who the bride will be.
2. Who are going to be attending the wedding? There are two selections Hebrews of Gentiles.
3. Where will the wedding be held? In the King's house. Heaven.
4. What attire will be worn? White is required.
5. When will this marriage occur? When the Wedding Feast is ready.

Verse 3 So, the king (God) starts His preparations for the feast by first sending out His servants (prophets) to invite selected individuals (Hebrews) to His son's wedding feast .However, they all rejected the invitation. (God son is rejected by Jews)

Verse 4 the King tries to get them to come by enticing them with the cuisine treasures He is preparing. But still, no one accepts the offer a second time.

In Verse 5–6, they make light of the invitation and go their own way. And those who remained took the messenger (Apostles) and treated them badly and killed those messengers

Verse 7 The king was truly angry at those murders and sent his army which destroyed them and burned up their city. (Jerusalem 70 BC)

Verse 8 The feast is ready but those invited were not worthy (Israel)

Verse 9 The king send his servants (Disciples and Missionaries) went out to invite (Gospel) anyone (Gentiles) to come and they did.

Verse 10 These servants did as commanded and many (Gentiles) were found, both the bad and the good, and many guest (Christians came to God).

Verse 11 When the king came to meet His guests, one did not wear a wedding garment (White robe "the righteous acts of the Saints") (left behind)

Verse 12 The king ask him why he was not dressed in White, and he was speechless (Lack of deeds) These are the Pew-sitters who have done nothing for the Kingdom of Jesus, NO Works. They are saved by faith but have no treasures. These I call the Tribulation Saints.

<u>Verse 13</u> They had this person tied up and cast into outer darkness where there will be weeping and gnashing of teeth. We have been taught this pertains to Hell, but this is not death. It is a place of punishment for both saved and unsaved individuals called The Great tribulation. God wrath on earth for seven years.

The Tribulation Saints must go through the Great Tribulation and perform <u>works for salvation</u>. ***This work is not accepting the Mark of the Beast.*** Those who reject the Mark will be beheaded Those who accept the mark will be promised food and water They are in the <u>Valley of Decision</u> to accept or reject the Mark of the Beast. To accept the Mark removes any possibility of salvation. At the first look, they are morally killed by Satan or spiritually killed by God. Seems to me spiritual death is not the one to miss.

There are a number of *clues* which I included in the passages. These verses show God total plan for salvation. God first revealed himself to the Hebrew people. They accepted God as the one true God. Then, all gods were singular, but this God is three Gods in one. This aspect of a triune God is rejected still today by the Israelites. They rejected Jesus and eventually had Jesus killed.

Because they are not in the Rapture, they will have to go through the Great Tribulation. This period is primarily for Israel's salvation. There 144,000 Hebrews (Israelites) will teach them of Jesus' Gospel and convert them to Jesus' salvation. No small task for the 140,000 during the seven years.

How did they get the knowledge of Jesus? This question has not been addressed, that I am aware. It is possible they come from Jews in our time who have converted to Jesus. And will have the mind of Jesus as will all Christians.

These have to be Jewish Christians as Rev. 7:3–8 tells they come from 12,000 from each of the 12 tribes of Israel.

LESSONS LEARNED

1. Christians will Wed with Jesus.
2. God has planned this wedding before the beginning of Creation.
3. He called the Hebrews first, but they rejected to come to Jesus.
4. Then God called the Gentiles though Jesus' apostles and the Jews killed them.
5. Then God sent Jesus, knowing they would kill Jesus
6. But this murder played into God's plan for salvation.
7. Jesus paid the Gentiles debt for sins they have committed. And covertly for the Hebrew sins also.
8. God Raptures the righteous into Heaven's Paradise.
9. God brings the seven years of great punishment on earth
10. Jews are converted to Jesus by 144,000 Jewish missionaries.
11. Jesus returns to destroy all evil. Satan is locked into the Abyss.
12. Jesus 1,000-year Kingdom is established.
13. After 1,000 years, Satan is released from the Abyss and creates a large army to destroy Jesus.
14. God burns up Satan's army instantly.
15. Satan is cast into the Lake of Fire
16. God's Great White Throne Judgment is completed. All lost souls are judged and cast t into the Lake of Fire forever.
17. God creates a New Heaven and a New Earth, and God's City comes to the New Earth
18. God's plan for man comes to fruition and eternity begins

✝ CHAPTER 21 ✎

The Cost of Discipleship

Luke 14:28–33

This can be a difficult condition to accept especially for a person who has enjoyed God's blessing of wealth. Remember the verse *"You cannot serve God and mammon?"*

Luke 14:28–33 (28) For which of you, intending to build a tower, <u>sitteth not down first, and counteth the cost,</u> whether he have sufficient **to finish** it? **(29) Lest haply, after he hath laid the foundation, and is not able to finish** it, all that behold it **begin to mock him, (30) Saying, This man began to build, and was not able to finish. (31) Or what king, going to make war against another king, sitteth not down first, and consulteth whether he be able with ten thousand to meet him that cometh against him with twenty thousand? (32) Or else, while the other is yet a great way off, he sendeth an ambassage, and desireth conditions of peace. <u>(33) So likewise, whosoever he be of you that forsaketh not all that he hath, he cannot be my disciple.</u>**

It will be difficult for a wealthy person to be able to give up everything and follow Jesus. Some good persons must come to the reality of their passion. The poorer the person and the less quantity and quality of positions, may find it easier to give up positions. So, pray for these types of wealthy individual as their heart is capture by their lust of the eyes, flesh. It indicates the condition of their heart.

Wealth is not evil in itself but can cause the love of money covertly. Just the thought of giving away all you have work for, the comforts, respect, security, and other pleasures; captures one, especially as one gets older. It is a profonde indication what is the most important in your life.

Also, it reveals the trust you lack in Jesus and God. God gave the wealth and can take it away. We looked at scripture that is imperative you remember if you face this problem.

Mark 8:36–37 *"(36) For what shall it profit a man, if he shall gain the whole world, and lose his soul? (37) Or what will a man give in exchange for his soul?"*

As you can no doubt see the aftereffects of greed to gain the whole world and die with and evil heart opposing Jesus. As I said before, it is not the blessing of God's providing wealth for a believer but the love for that wealth above the love of God and Jesus.

The time is coming where wealth will be taken away from the wealthy believers. Due to Satan's requirement to accept his Mark of the Beast. To retain your wealth, you will have to take the Mark of the Beast and give your soul to Satan. Thereby, condemning yourself to the Lake of Fire.

There is also, verses that explain the difficulty of a rich person to be save, and it is found in Mark 10.17–27. A wealthy young man came running to Jesus and asked, *"what shall I do that I may inherit eternal life?"*

Jesus' answer was, *"sell whatsoever thou hast, and give it to the poor,--- then come and follow me.* The young rich man went away grieving.

The disciples asked, *"Who then can be saved."* Jesus' answer was *"With men it is impossible, but with God all things are possible."* What is the measurement to determine wealth? Some God gives wealth like Solomon. But many are given poverty like Lazarus.

Some Christians can properly handle wealth, and some cannot. Remember, money is the root of all evil and You cannot serve God and Mammon (money).

What think ye of Jesus' answer?

Matthew 19:23–24 "*(23) Then said Jesus unto his disciples, Verily I say unto you, That a rich man shall hardly enter into the kingdom of heaven. (24) And again I say unto you, It is easier for a camel to go through the eye of a needle, than for a rich man to enter into the kingdom of God.*

Jerusalem had a narrow gate called "**the Needle.** " It was so small that a merchant had unload his merchandise for the camel to get through that gate, to get into Jerusalem. Jesus is revealing a metaphor of the rich must unload their care for merchandise to get access into Jesus' city (Kingdom's Capital).

Can you imagine the thieves that gathered at this gate waiting for a careless individual who they could rob? If only one merchant without help, these thieves could rob the merchandise while he and the camel is going through the Eye of the Needle to get the other side. And then return to no merchandise. And also lose the camel he just left in Jerusalem.

This reveals the care a Richman must consider every day. There is not much time to spend in prayer with God. Example: if you won a million dollars what would you need to do to protect that treasure.

How would you transport that cash to a protected financial agency? What is the limit of funds protected in the agency? You may need to divert other funs to other agencies to have government insurance coverage. How will you handle all the phone calls for business opportunities? What investments are legal and how would you check them out. Who would you select for advice and what is the proper cost? Then you will need a last Will and Testament. Fake Law suites to payoff are lawyer fees. Scammers and others trying to get some of you treasure. And a lot of so-called friends. The more you make the more you will spend on protections you will need for you and your loved ones.

I am exhausted just thinking of all this work. Be careful what you wish for, you just may get it.

CHAPTER 22

Coming of God's' City

Pre-scripture Information

I want you first to read about this eternal city that will come to earth after creating the New Universe and the New Earth. Due to all the bloodshed on the planet, God wants to give all righteous souls, and necessary for God himself to be present on an unstained world or planet. Therefore, his home will be pure, clean, untainted by death, as Death has been destroyed. This earth is God's and our eternal Home. It will be a great deal more pleasant than the now present earth. As you read, keep in mind that the construction is to God as common building materials. Notice the streets are made of pure gold. So pure it is transparency, and that is basic pavement.

Revelation 21:10—26 *"(10) And he carried me away in the spirit to a great and high mountain, and shewed me that great city, the holy Jerusalem, descending out of heaven from God, (11) Having the glory of God: and her light was like unto a stone most precious, even like a jasper stone, clear as crystal; (12)And had a wall great and high, and had twelve gates, and at the gates twelve angels, and names written thereon, which are the names of the twelve tribes of the children of Israel: (13) On the east three gates; on the north three gates; on the south three gates; and on the west three gates. (14) And the wall of the city had twelve foundations, and in them the names of the twelve apostles of the Lamb. (15) And he that talked with me had a golden* *reed to measure the city, and the gates thereof, and the wall thereof. (16) And the <u>city lieth foursquare</u>, and the <u>length is as large as the breadth</u>: and he <u>measured the city with the reed, twelve thousand furlongs. The length and the breadth and the height of it are equal.</u> (17) And he measured the wall thereof, an hundred* and *forty* and *four cubits,* according to **the measure of a man, that is, of the angel.** *(18) And the building of the wall of it was* of **jasper: and the city** was **pure gold, like unto clear glass.** *(19) And the foundations of the wall of the city* were **garnished with all manner of precious stones. The first foundation was** *jasper; the second, sapphire; the third, a chalcedony; the fourth, an emerald; (20) The fifth, sardonyx; the sixth, sardius; the seventh, chrysolite; the eighth, beryl; the ninth, a topaz; the tenth, a chrysoprasus; the eleventh, a jacinth; the twelfth, an amethyst. (21) And the twelve gates* were *twelve pearls; every several gates was of one pearl: and the street of the city* was **pure gold, as it were transparent glass.** *(22) And <u>I saw no temple therein: for the Lord God Almighty and the Lamb are the temple of it. (23) And the city had no need of the sun, neither of the moon, to shine in it: for the glory of God did lighten it, and the Lamb</u>* is *<u>the light thereof. (24) And the nations of them which are saved shall walk in the light of it: and the kings of the earth do bring their glory and honour into it.</u> (25) And the gates of it shall not be shut at all by day: for there shall be no night there. (26) And they shall bring the glory and honour of the nations into it."*

How can we humans conceive of the beauty and majesty of such a place? Breathtaking beauty everywhere we look, and this beauty will never be boring. Just for a second, let us see only the magnitude of the size of the city.

In <u>verse 16,</u> God reveals the city is a cube with equal length on all sides. The width is 1400 miles, the depth is 1400 miles, and the height 1400 miles. These are miles, not feet or kilometers. If you convert this to volume, there are 2,744,000,000 *miles inside the city.* If we want to know the square feet per floor, it is 10,348,800,000 sqft. If you want to see the number of 10-foot stories, it is 739,200 floors. If you want to know how many 3,000 square feet apartments per floor, it is 3,449,600 apartments. And lastly, if you desire the complete apartments in the city, it is 2,549,944,320,000 total for a 3,000 sqft apartment in this city of God. *Is this not a mansion?*

In verse 22, there will be no need for the Temple of God because God and Jesus will be present with us forever. Also, we see there will be kings who will bring their glory to this city, and it is an open city that never closes; availability is 24/7. An exception is found in Rev. 21:27.

Revelation 21:27 *"And there shall in no wise enter into it anything that defileth, neither* whatsoever worketh abomination, nor maketh a lie: but they which are written in the Lamb's book of life."

This verse is a *clue* because all evil on earth has been before the *Great Throne Judgment of God*, and they are found guilty and cast into the Lake of Fire. Its location is unknown, but it is extremely far away from God's city. This statement is assuring us that there is nothing for us to fear in Heaven.

INSIDE THE CITY OF GOD.

Revelation 22:1–5 *"(1) And he shewed me a pure river of water of life, clear as crystal, proceeding out of the throne of God and of the Lamb. (2) In the midst of the street of it, and on either side of the river,* was there the tree of life, which bare twelve manner of fruits, and yielded her fruit every month: and the leaves of the tree were for the healing of the nations. (3) And there shall be no more curse: but the throne of God and of the Lamb shall be in it; and his servants shall serve him: (4) And they shall see his face; and his name shall be in their foreheads. (5) And there shall be no night there; and they*

need no candle, neither light of the sun; for the Lord God giveth them light: and they shall reign for ever and ever."

These verses reveal the Eternal City of God, of which we have studied the enormous size previously. This new city's location is at Jerusalem on the New Earth; therefore, the New Earth must be gigantic to contain the past's righteous souls to this writing's future. The population will include the prelaw (10 commandments plus Torah) Old Testament Saints, *who are saved by God's grace through their love of God and their attempt to do uncommanded good.* God is evaluating their heart to see or reveal; we are evil bent from Adam's failure to obey. *The Law will not judge this group of Old Testament Saints,* but the law will judge all that comes after the Law. We see this in Rom.2.

Romans 2:5-13 *"(2) But after thy hardness and impenitent heart treasurest up unto thyself wrath against the day of wrath and revelation of the righteous judgment of God; (6) Who will render to every man according to his deeds: (7) To them who by patient continuance in well doing seek for glory and honour and immortality, eternal life: (8) But unto them that are contentious, and do not obey the truth, but obey unrighteousness, indignation and wrath, (9) Tribulation and anguish, upon every soul of man that doeth evil, of the Jew first, and also of the Gentile; (10) But glory, honour, and peace, to every man that worketh good, to the Jew first, and also to the Gentile: (11) For there is no respect of persons with God. (12) For as many as have sinned without law shall also perish without law: and as many as have sinned in the law shall be judged by the law; (13) For not the hearers of the law are just before God, but the doers of the law shall be justified".*

In verse 2, notice the primary consideration for God's grace to be applied is in a person's attitude of their heart. *Hardness* and an *unrepentant heart* are the dominant negative attitude that will affect God's will to exercise his grace for salvation. God knows he has given us an impossible task to perform. Therefore, he has given to those who try to please God; they will be given grace unto salvation. Those who do not attempt to please will be cast into Tribulation (punishment) for the evil they choose over good.

Old Testament Saint Before the Law

In <u>verse 12,</u> we see an interesting statement from God.

"(12) For as many as have sinned without law shall also perish without law: and as many as have sinned in the law shall be judged by the law;"

Here is a dividing point *clue*, those who *die without the law* and those *who die with the law*. After Adam's fall, the only guidance these people had was the Knowledge of Good and Evil. God wanted them to learn to exercise their own self-will to do good. Just as God does good, but God knew they would fail, but he needed to provide justice for those who made a sincere effort --- Grace. THEY WOULD DIE WITHOUT THE LAW TO JUDGE THEM. Therefore, it was in their deeds to please God that proved their loyalty to God. If God is a just God (and he is), he will not punish those who had no law to be judged by that unseen law. These I call the *Pre-Law Old Testament Saints.*

LAW AND OLD TESTAMENT SAINTS

Those individuals who <u>did not</u> exercise their self-will for good proved their disloyalty to God and their lack of desire to please God. This condition was and is still unacceptable to God. This relationship between good and evil is the foundation for man's use of his free self-will. We are given our permission by God to exercise our self-will without his active interference. But he will send the Holy Spirit to attempt to change that person's mind. But it is that individual's right to perform actions to his weak desires. However, God will provide for the victims of that person's failure to exercise good, and payment for that act of evil is required. Nobody and I mean nobody, will get away with evil behavior. They can be eternally forgiven, but repentance must occur on earth before death; God calls this his chastisement.

We Christians are to; pray for their *eternal forgiveness* but insist on their earthly punishment, but with mercy. *Spare the rod, spoil the child* (Pro.13:24). A rod is a tool for discipline in the Bible, and it is referred to 86 times. For us, humans, most of us seem to learn by pain. Touching a hot stove is one example. *But the rod is not for brutality*. Today in our society, many parents *have not taught* their children punishment for disobedience to their parents, police, or other adults. They have, in effect, have relegated their responsibility to the police and the court system. This system has more significant impacts on their children's lives than a correct spanking. A young child needs to learn self-control at an early stage in life. We see an increase in bullying today, child felony crimes, drug users becoming younger and younger, drug pusher younger, an inability to deal with disappointments, and more incredible yet disrespect for parents. It is the parent's or parent's responsibility to bring up a child to respond correctly to their society. The Bible is clear on this fact. In the Old Testament Law, God said that an incorrigible child (cursed his mother and father) was to be put to death **Lev. 19:9.** Therefore, it behooves mothers and fathers to train children early in their life to deal with the experiences they will meet in adulthood. Adult Jobs are not based on participation but performance.

Note

Children can learn to deal with failure or disappointment at an early age. But, if this ability to deal with the problems at an early age is not addressed, it will result in anger during adulthood. Also, the Bible says, "SPARE THE ROD AND SPOIL THE CHILD." If parents do not chastise the child for unacceptable behavior, they leave that job to the police.

We are experiencing this symptom today with President Trump (Republican) by the spoiled Democratic Party members who were not taught how to deal with disappointment.

I did not make the baseball team the first time. So, I learned the lesson and practiced more, and made the team the next tryout. I did not get a trophy for just participating in a tournament game when we lost. Next year we practice removing our play mistakes or weakness. And the following year, that trophy really meant something to us. We learned how to deal with disappointments correctly. Our psyche was simply fine.

Life in the real world as an adult is like sports; if you do not perform the best, you are removed from the team (Job). We are rewarded for our success and not for participation.

There will be those *Old Testament Saints* from the Law period who tried to follow the law as best they could. This transition point now gives the deed requirements and the punishment as a measuring tool for righteousness. And they also found grace in God's eyes in their sincere efforts. This Law from God revealed that they and all Saints cannot perfectly keep all the laws. The sin nature given to us by Adam's failure is such an evil force, we cannot overcome entirely. Only the Messiah, the son of God, will be capable of keeping all of God's laws perfectly. **God's grace is the prime factor in salvation.** *These Old Testament Saints, who believed in God and tried to perform the deeds of the law, are saved by God's grace.* So, God reveals to us today his mercy through his Grace, and we too must exercise mercies for our fellow man, especially considering their eternal death.

So, we see two types of Old Testament Saints, Pre-Law and Post Law. Jesus did not remove the Law but fulfilled the Law for man. *This transition brought in the period of Faith only for salvation.* Faith is the ultimate mercy for the weakness God permitted to be inserted into man through Adam's self-will. This insertion is a significant turning point in

God's plan for man. Those individuals, who believe God's son paid our debt of sin, rose from the grave, and will come again for Christians, are saved by <u>Faith Alone</u>. This faith appeared to break the Deeds needed for salvation, and it did. But Deeds now take on a different importance from salvation. Jesus tells us to store up Treasures in Heaven in Mat. 6.

Matthew 6:19–21 *"(19) Lay not up for yourselves treasures upon earth, where moth and rust doth corrupt, and where thieves break through and steal: (20) But lay up for yourselves treasures in heaven, where neither moth nor rust doth corrupt, and where thieves do not break through nor steal: (21) For where your treasure is, there will your heart be also.:"*

What is a treasure to God? We cannot imagine what a treasure is to God. For us, we think of financial gain of some sort. But God made all the financial treasures, and they are not unique to him. He does not need money; if he did, he would speak it into existence. So, what is a Treasure? Unknown at this time! But it must be fantastic. And how do we get this unique treasure? By DEEDS! Now we see the change of deeds for salvation to a different importance but still required for Treasures. To store up infers deeds. To store up is a physical or spiritual action on man's part. Jesus gave us numerous verses of scriptures as to *what we are to PERFORM.*

Matthew chapters 5, 6, and 7 are dedicated to actions and deeds we are to perform. The most excellent acts are found in Matthew 28:18–20, The Great Commission. I must reveal that this is not a commission but a Command of Jesus, our King. The commission is a less powerful word than Command. So human nature takes control and makes this not too important. However, the beatitudes are what we are to strive for, but the Great Command is our requirement to perform. *Failure to perform this command in some form will not give you treasures.* Therefore, a question comes to mind; if you have faith in Jesus but perform no deeds, are you saved? YES, for this is spoken of in **Rom.5:1.** So how is this tied together, Deeds and Faith?

First, let us look into the Church. The Church is the true believer in Jesus for salvation. Some will perform the deeds, and some will sit in the pews and do nothing to build Jesus' Kingdom but worship. These are the deedless saved who will need to do deeds for treasures. *They have lost the treasure of the Rapture* and now will be required to do deeds during the most horrible of times on earth. <u>*There is only one deed they must perform, and that deed is not to accept the Mark of the Beast.*</u> To receive this Mark, removes any possibilities for salvation, and their destination is the Lake of Fire. Those that reject the Mark, I call the *Tribulation Saints*. They kept their Faith and now must gain treasures. The only deed they must do is, reject the Mark of the Beast.

Both Pre-Law, Post Law Old Testament Saints, and Tribulation Saints are taken to Jesus in the 1st Harvest (a treasure), completed just before the War #1 Armageddon Rev. 14. Here is when Jesus' Kingdom headquarters will be in Jerusalem.

Our eternal home, the city of God, is waiting for our entrance. It is impossible to grasp the experience we will share there; words will fail.

LESSONS LEARNED

1. The city of God comes to earth after the *New Earth* is created.
2. It is an extremely large city.
3. God and Jesus will be the light for that city.
4. Nothing evil will ever inter this city or earth.
5. The city's occupants are God, Jesus, the Holy Spirit, the Church Saints (Christians the Bride of Christ), Tribulation Saints, the Old Testament Saints, and angels.
6. Do not store up earthly treasures but heavenly treasures.

7. Righteous deeds are the treasures to store up. You will enjoy them forever.
8. Children must be brought up in the Lord by parents. Do not leave this to the government. Sometimes reasonable pain is necessary.
9. The seven-year Tribulation will come on earth.
10. For the Tribulation Saints, *must reject the Mark of the Beast* to be included in the 1st Harvest.

Sometimes the Bible seems so depressing and not as uplifting as we would like. Remember, sweet words (itchy ear) very often come from Satan. God knows Heaven is an experience that we cannot understand. In time Heaven will reveal itself, but so will the Lake of Fire. At times, God is more concerned with you, knowing the elements *that will prevent you from the eternal experience of Heaven.* Also, as Christians, we are to learn as much as possible about the Words of God. We read God's desires for this in 2nd Tim.2:15.

2nd Timothy 2:15 *"Study to shew thyself* approved *unto God, a workman that needeth not to be ashamed, rightly dividing the word of truth."*

Motivation is important to God. It reveals the condition of our hearts. We saw in the letter to the Church of the Laodiceans the lack of motivation for the lost. The heart fuels motivation. We see this in people's reactions in an emergency. The heart fires the brain to produce adrenalin, which energizes us into actions even for strangers. We are motivated by knowing the results of what is going to happen. Love for a family member in peril motivates us very quickly. But, what if a stranger?

Today we see events that de-motivate us from helping a person in need. The Good Samaritan Law was passed to protect doctors and others from greedy individuals. Kidnapping on highways, giving help on roads, using restrooms at rest stops, and other events frighten us. It is hard to be a good Samaritan, which also reveals our lack of trust in God. Jesus tells us of this time in Mat. 10.

Matthew 10:16 *"Behold, I send you forth as sheep in the midst of wolves: be ye therefore wise as serpents, and harmless as doves."*

While this is scripture is in the dissertation of Christians' future persecutions, it is still good everyday advice. Think before you act, if possible. Listen and feel for the Holy Spirit leading. Ask God.

As time approaches near the Rapture, great evil will be revealed on earth. Christians should recognize His nearness by foretold prophecies. One is the downfall of governments. America the last bastions of freedom and is in the sights of evil control. America is the final reflection of Jesus. When the last Child of God is removed (Rapture), there will be many left behind. Life on earth for righteous people will be horrendous. Satan will be in control, and righteous people will be sought after and destroyed.

All so far is death and destruction. But this God last love letter to you and me. His loved is revealed in his tell us so that we can spare ourselves the pain and distress coming to evil. For Christians we will be in Heaven as specters with the mind of Christ.

We are removed from God's wrath. The punishments revealed are just to us then. No remorse for lost souls receiving what they themselves caused after waning and warnings. They have blasphemed the Holy Spirit for the last time.

God must keep his covenants with us and Israel and reward us for reasonable service. God must now destroy his evil children He loved so much He sent His son to die for them and us. What more must God do to win our love for Him? I pray we can see the warm love through tough love.

My Closing Prayer

God Bless You and Keep You.

God Bless Your Family.

God Bless Our Military.

God Bless Our Police.

God Bless Our Missionaries.

God Bless Our Country.

God Bless Our Family and Friends.

Love in Christ Jesus.

Tommy Bruce Jones

SUPPORTING SOURCES

1. "Strong's Exhaustive Concordance," Copyright 1890 by Mr. James Strong, Madison, N.J. Printed by Crusade Bible Publishers, INC. Box 90011, Nashville TN 37209
2. "Funk and Wagnall Standard Desk Dictionary," Funk and Wagnall Corporation, Harp & Row, Publishers Inc. All rights reserved except in case of Brief Quotations embodied in critical articles and reviews.
3. All scriptures are from the King James Bible, © Copyright 1957 by Frank Charles Thompson, published by B.B. Kirkbridge Bible Co. Inc. Indianapolis, Ind. 41 Reprint: All rights reserved.
4. All quoted scriptures are from the Holy Bible, King James Version Cambridge Addition: 1769; King James Bible Online www.kingjamesbibleonline.org.
5. Photo of the old Cathedral is by Mr. Harry Smith, #2886268 at www.harrysmith321.hs@gmail.com
6. Photo of the stone wall is by Mr. Paul Zoetemeijer at www. unsplash.com.

www.ingramcontent.com/pod-product-compliance
Lightning Source LLC
Chambersburg PA
CBHW071356120626
46546CB00002B/709